IM PRESS

АЛЕКСАНДР ВЕЙЦМАН

ДЕМОГРАФИЯ ДРЕМЛЮЩИХ ДУШ

Перевод на английский
Лоренса Богослава

Бостон • 2022 • Чикаго

ALEXANDER VEYTSMAN

A SUCCESSION
OF SOMNOLENT
SOULS

Translated into English
By Laurence Bogoslaw

BOSTON • 2022 • Chicago

Alexander Veytsman
A Succession of Somnolent Souls

Александр Вейцман
Демография дремлющих душ

ISBN 978-1-950319-87-9

Library of Congress Control Number: 2022946286

Translated into English by Laurence Bogoslaw

Cover Illustration by iStock/bestdesigns

Published by M•Graphics | Boston, MA
 ☐ www.mgraphics-books.com
 ✉ mgraphics.books@gmail.com

In cooperation with Bagriy & Company | Chicago, IL
 ☐ www.bagriycompany.com
 ✉ printbookru@gmail.com

Printed in the United States of America

СОДЕРЖАНИЕ

CONTENTS

ОТ АВТОРА

Когда Лэрри Богослав предложил перевести несколько моих стихотворений на английский язык, я пообещал ему, что буду следовать двум простым правилам: не вмешиваться в процесс перевода и быть благодарным. Поскольку стихотворный жанр по большому счёту мало кому нужен, а людей, которых интересует нечто рифмообразное, становится всё меньше, то именно молчание и благодарность представляются мне наиболее надёжным модусом операнди не только между автором и переводчиком, но и в рамках окружающего мира, куда направлены те или иные строки.

Я благодарен Лэрри.

Я благодарен Анатолию Розенцвейгу за бесценные советы в русских оригиналах.

Я благодарен журналам, где в разные годы были напечатаны стихотворения из настоящей книги, среди них: «Балкон», «День и ночь», «Дети Ра», «Дружба народов», «Зарубежные записки», «Зинзивер», «Интерпоэзия», «Новый журнал», «Новая юность», «Слово/Word», «Стороны света» и *EastWest Literary Forum*.

Я благодарен всем, кого люблю.

Александр Вейцман
14 августа 2022

TRANSLATOR'S INTRODUCTION

Laurence H. Bogoslaw

The finest aesthetic moments contain a sense of wonder: a recognition of something great emerging from a unique, unrepeatable set of elements. I experienced such a moment when Alexander Veytsman read one of his original works in an intimate space at Poets House in New York City in 2015, during the presentation of the Compass Poetry Translation Awards. This poem was inspiring in two ways. First, it affirmed the abiding value of the written word to preserve art and memory; and second, it contained a challenge I could not resist. When I heard the lines:

> а Моцарт в птичьей гамме
> летит, попутно рассекая облака

[a Mótsart v ptíchei gámme / letít, popútno rassekáya oblaká]
(literally: and Mozart in the scale of birds / flies, slicing through clouds on the way)

...I was transported to the pastoral scene of Fyodor Tyutchev's 1830 poem "Vesennyaya groza" (Spring Tempest), which contains the line *В лесу не молкнет птичий гам* [V lesú ne mólknet ptíchii gam] ("in the forest the din of birds does not fall silent"). With just one added syllable — *gam* to *gamma* (musical scale) — Veytsman had brought together two eras, two nations, two forms of art. My thought at this moment was: "How impossible to translate!" — followed immediately by: "How necessary to translate!"

After the reading, I asked Veytsman to consider letting me try. He graciously consented, emailing me a Word copy of his entire 2011 collection. So it was that in the summer of 2015, I began the process of delving into the mysteries that lie at the heart of Veytsman's meticulously crafted poems. Since then, with his constant encouragement and consultation, I have drafted at least rough English versions of nearly every work in that collection, as well as several poems he has published since then. He and I have been in regular contact by email and phone, exchanging drafts, questions, comments, and answers.

Veytsman himself set no parameters for how his poems should be approached. For example, he gave me total choice in poetic structure, as he recognizes that free verse has long been the standard for English poetry, and he himself writes free verse in English. However, the choice was obvious to me from the beginning that the translated poems should follow the meter and rhyme of the original.

I realize that this choice goes against the modern poetic tradition, not only for original works but for translations as well. In the 1980s, Robert Bly made an argument in *The Eight Stages of Translation* that has stood the test of time: poetry translated into American English should follow the tone, diction and style of contemporary English. In our era, he wrote, poetic diction no longer uses the "high" or "aristocratic" style that English literature of past centuries used to have.

All language has two levels at least: an upper and a lower. We recognize the "upper" in Shakespeare's sonnets: language high-flown, ethical, elaborated, capable of concept, witty, dignified, noble in tone. We might speculate that in the American language now only the "lower" level is alive. It flows along on earth; it is a physical language that everyone contributes to, warm, intense, with short words, well connected to the senses, musical, capable of feeling. This sensual language is the only one we have... William Carlos Williams used this language by principle... In America the "noble" stream dried out around 1900, against the will of Henry James, and since that time, as Williams declared, the writer has had no choice. (Bly 1982: 79)

However, the idea that poetry should sound warm, intense and sensual does not mean that verses from other languages should be translated as prose. In fact, Bly himself wrote that a translator should internalize the rhythms and sounds of the original in order to make the English version musical. I would argue that even poetry translators who claim to privilege "content" over "form" (Bly did not fall into this trap) also seek to preserve something of the elegance and harmony of the original. There are many possibilities here: syntactic parallelism, lexical cohesion (including repetitions of words and phrases), internal rhyme and near-rhyme, vowel harmony, alliteration, and much more. These elements are never completely ignored.

Therefore, one might ask: with all of these poetic devices at my disposal, why impose the additional strictures of rhyme schemes and metrical forms? The answer is twofold. First, when translating any work (prose, poetry, song) I try to do justice to the original poet's technical expertise, which in Veytsman's case is considerable. Even if my poetic product does not measure up to his achievement, I consider it my duty as a translator (as well as a great pleasure) to pursue the *process* of making poetry: seeking the most precise phrasing, the most moving rhythm, trying out fresh possibilities over and over again until the poem sounds right. Second, Veytsman's choice to use canonical rhyme and meter in itself attests to his reverence for the Russian poetic tradition. To discard those compositional elements would be to discard part of Veytsman's role in that tradition.

13

The cases where I relax these standards are those in which the poet does so himself: for example, Veytsman sometimes writes stanzas with varied line patterns (mixing trimeters, tetrameters, pentameters, and longer measures), uses accentual verse (dolniks) instead of uniform feet, opts for near-rhymes, and occasionally mixes in irregular rhyme schemes.

Going back to the question of tone, in my pursuit of equivalent rhyme and meter I have done my best to match Veytsman's verbal style as well — or rather his variety of styles, which range from casually conversational ("Fall 2008," "One More Email to the State of Chaos") to ritualistically formal ("Cavafy's Monologue"). At times I have intentionally strayed into the realm of contrived syntax and lexical choices for the sake of reproducing the original wordplay. For example, in "Battery Park City," the poet Gumilyov adds his "train of thought to the train of clouds" (my attempt to preserve Veytsman's repetition of *khod* "movement") and various forms of "to be" weave alliteratively with the names Bunin and Bach in "Rue de Rennes."

An entirely different dimension of Veytsman's poetry is his imagery, which is often rooted in history, visual art, history, music. These images are not always self-explanatory to the non-Russian reader, and thus the motivation for using them is not necessarily clear in translation. Rather than try to articulate some overarching principle of how far to go in "domesticating" or "foreignizing" a given image or allusion (to cite Lawrence Venuti's famous dichotomy), I will present a narrative of how a line-by-line "prose" translation (more or less what I started with for every poem) became transformed through a recursive process of close reading, appreciation of poetic structure, analysis of lexical meaning, and research on extratextual references. I will begin with the aforementioned poem that drew me into Veytsman's work; please refer to the Russian original on page 144.

Now Pushkin writes in smooth iambs that "Some
are no more, and others afar."
Now Stalin thinks again of *The Turbins*
to go out [and see] on a free evening.
Now Richter in Salzburg plays "WTC,"
and Mozart in the scale of birds
flies, slicing through clouds on the way,
and weeps with the clouds.

Let's go to dinner, dear friend, and recall everyone
who is mentioned above.
You wrote them letters at some time — which is no sin,
but a way to survive in a niche.
Perhaps the mystery of the soul and of the trade
is kept not in speech, [but] on paper,
like part of the force that forever wishes ill,
but accomplishes good.

The quotation from Pushkin is familiar to Russians, who know it from his novel in verse *Eugene Onegin*; it is a wistful reminder of the poet's contemporaries who were executed or exiled in the wake of the Decembrist Revolution of 1825. The literary allusion is rich and meaningful, but in this case I left it to curious readers to seek out the significance for themselves.

For the Stalin reference, however, I felt that readers needed more help. Here is the backstory that I gleaned from correspondence with Veytsman and my own research: Bulgakov's play *The Days of the Turbins* opened in 1926, but was soon canceled under criticism by the Soviet press. It was only through Stalin's direct intervention that it reopened in 1932, running until 1941. The Soviet leader is said to have seen it many times. An additional subtext that impacted my English phrasing is that the play's protagonists are an anti-revolutionary family in Ukraine during the Soviet Civil War. To highlight the odd irony of Stalin's fondness for this work, I replaced the name "Turbins" (which most English readers would not know to stress on the second syllable, anyway) with the more familiar "White Guards," from the title of Bulgakov's novel on which he based the play.

Where the poem alludes to Soviet pianist Stanislav Richter, I partially expanded the name of the Bach piece *The Well-Tempered Clavier* — for three reasons. First was the difficulty of fitting the abbreviation "WTC" into iambic meter. Second is the issue of familiarity: while Veytsman's musical background allows him to know famous pieces by their initials, most English speakers, even classical music buffs, do not. The third and most important motivation: "tempered" offered a convenient near-rhyme for "tempest," the subject of the Tyutchev poem mentioned above.

However, to make the Tyutchev reference not simply known, but thematically meaningful, to the intended reader, some space had to be created in the translation. Here is where the richness of our English verb stock came to the rescue. I found that the image of Mozart flying upward through the clouds could be conveyed succinctly by having him "scale" the clouds. Fortuitously (and to my mind, miraculously), its noun form also extends to the musical semantic field. This dual-purpose word gave me the length of an entire six-beat line to paraphrase Tyutchev — "like birds that keep on singing in a springtime tempest." I considered it crucial to reinforce the theme that Veytsman offers later in the poem: the persistence of art in the face of oppositional forces.

The second stanza presented challenges that were superficial by comparison: mainly vocabulary shifts to accommodate Veytsman's rhyme scheme (AbAbCdCd) and metrical structure (alternating lines of iambic hexameter and trimeter). The most glaring *otsebyatina* (to borrow the term used by Russian critics to condemn translators' inventions) was "classic and romantic," to rhyme with a phrase two lines later that I could not do without: "survival tactic." Almost no other thematic content had to be changed, although I did allow myself to expand some of Veytsman's trimeter lines to four beats. Here is my final version of the poem:

As Pushkin writes in smooth iambic verse: "Some are
no more, and others far away."
Now Stalin thinks of going out to see White Guards
again after a busy day.
And Richter plays in Salzburg, his technique well tempered,
and Mozart scales the clouds
like birds that keep on singing in a springtime tempest
and weeps among the clouds.

Let's go and dine, dear friend, and then we will recall
each one, the classic and romantic.
You used to write them letters, which is no sin at all —
it's a survival tactic.
The mysteries of the soul, the secrets of the guild
may not be told aloud, but could
be kept on paper, like a force that always wishes ill
but ends up doing good.

Veytsman's allusions often venture beyond Russia into other literary realms. For example, his poetic narrator swims through a cove in Puerto Rico and imagines a mythic underworld beneath the surface populated by ancient Greek scholars. A plain translation of the Russian lines looks like this:

And onward — gazes fated never to see the light...
And ears that hear just one
And the same thing: from Plato, Diogenes.
And the profile of Ptolemy,
And the silhouette of Euclid.

These juxtapositions seem unmotivated, even to American readers well versed in literature (I asked a few), so I searched the annals of literature to discover some connection. I found that all of these figures are named in Canto IV of Dante's *Inferno*, along with the central figure of Aristotle, denoted by the Italian phrase "maestro di color che sanno" (master of those who know). In my translation, I offer readers the added hint of Dante's words, as well as explicit connections between the named philosophers:

And ears attuned to the master of those who know
who learned from Plato and Diogenes
and charted the course to Euclid and Ptolemy.

The above examples of allusion in Veytsman are not isolated cases; they are integral to his poetic sensibility. They are cultural signposts that guide the reader's perspective through continents, lifetimes, historical eras. Proust watches over a Boston library; verses from Tarkovsky cast their glow over an East Coast road trip; the heroine of Pushkin's "Queen of Spades" totters up a staircase on New York's Upper East Side.

When faced with allusions from Soviet history or Russian language and culture, I generally tried to add information to the English translations to make them more accessible. However, in a few cases Veytsman and I deemed it too intrusive to force these elements into the poems, and (unlike Nabokov in his translation of *Eugene Onegin*) we decided not to insert footnotes either. For the benefit of curious readers, I include these annotations here:

In the third of the "Three Studies" ("January Elegy"): The Russian pronouns *ty* and *vy* are used as informal and formal terms of address, respectively.

In the first of the "Moscow Excerpts": The mention of "Dr. Kukotsky" is an oblique reference to *The Kukotsky Enigma* (Kazus Kukotskogo), a novel by Lyudmila Ulitskaya that won the 2001 Booker Prize and was later made into a TV series, which aired in Russia in 2005.

In the poem beginning "Do you remember our old school": The "twenty-eight awesome heroes" were a group of soldiers from the Red Army's 316th Rifle Division who, according to official Soviet history, were killed in action during the Battle of Moscow (November 1941) after destroying 18 German tanks and stopping an enemy attack.

References like these require minimal research, but in cases where Veytsman's allusions have a broader reach — especially across artistic genres — they led me to enriching multimedia experiences as I worked through draft translations. The poem "A Summer in Parentheses," for example, presents a synesthetic experience of Chopin's Nocturne in E Major skimming over the Hudson River — and I listened to that nocturne over and over until its rhythms pervaded the lines. For other poems, I pored over paintings of Miró and Modigliani, and watched Alexander Nevsky's Battle on the Ice as filmed by Eisenstein. "Maria Yudina" — a poem about an artist's sketch of a musician's performance — spurred a variety of explorations. I listened to old recordings of Yudina playing Skriabin and Bartók; read stories and reminiscences about her career, including the legend about a hastily assembled midnight recording session of Mozart's Concerto

23 in A Major (an event portrayed in the opening scene of Armando Iannucci's 2017 film *The Death of Stalin*); and even, on Veytsman's suggestion, studied a documentary about her life, searching for the image of the sketch that inspired the poem.

Sometimes my research yields more than expected, uncovering a palimpsest of cultural artifacts (excuse the academic metaphor). For example, in Veytsman's poem "Invention," an unnamed artist experiences an intimate moment of communion with his deity. My unadorned draft translation read as follows: "He uttered 'Avva Otche' like Pasternak." The doubled epithet for "Father" in Hebrew and Old Church Slavonic is enough for an educated Russian reader to recall one of the most famous Dr. Zhivago poems, "Hamlet," in which the speaker asks God to spare him a tragic, early death. Pasternak in turn was alluding to the prayer that Jesus offered up in the garden of Gethsemane (Matthew 26:39): "O Father, may this cup pass from me." In my English translation of the Veytsman line, I decided to make the two-layered reference more transparent, including by changing the verb: "He prayed like Pasternak for the cup to pass."

In other cases, my research fails to do justice to the original. A prominent example is "An Italian Sketch," which replicates scenes and characters from Aleksei N. Tolstoy's celebrated children's tale *Buratino* (1936), itself an adaptation of Carlo Collodi's *Pinocchio*. To inform this translation, I dutifully reviewed excerpts from Tolstoy's story to familiarize myself with the characters and plot. This background knowledge prompted a few additions and adjustments to my rough translation, but several elements did not seem to fit. What is theater director Vsevolod Meyerhold doing in the second stanza? What about the reference to a national anthem in the fourth stanza, and Soviet state security in the fifth? And most importantly, why does the entire action of the poem take place on the Isle of Capri, which is not identified in Collodi's story or Tolstoy's adaptation?

It turns out that Veytsman was invoking *Buratino* not as a nostalgic relic of children's literature (although the poem is dedicated to his children) but as an allegory to Soviet history. Many Russian readers have interpreted this work as a *roman à clef* that retells a famous series of events from the early Soviet years, when the writer Maksim Gorky, who had fled the USSR to Capri in 1922, was "lured back" (Veytsman's words) by Stalin with the promise of renown as a great writer. (The promise came true: Gorky eventually became a living symbol of proletarian literature.) According to unofficial theories, which were never confirmed by Tolstoy himself, characters in *Buratino* are stand-ins for figures from the literary world. The "good" and "bad" puppet masters, Papa Carlo and Karabas-Barabas, respectively represent Konstantin Stanislavsky, longtime head of the Moscow Art Theater, and Meyerhold, who founded a new-generation theater under his own name. Basilio the cat and Alisa the fox, who kidnap and rob the wooden boy Buratino, represent unscrupulous literary agents who cheated Gorky out of royalties from his early stories and plays. And the title character represents Gorky himself.

Most of these details did not figure explicitly into my translation, but the overall themes of exile, deception, compulsion, and patriotism influenced my choices strongly — especially at the end, where the poetic narrator describes the creation of a new country. In our correspondence, Veytsman also wrote that Stalin's overtures to Gorky were part of a more widespread effort to bring Russian émigrés back to the Soviet Union. This note led me to make significant changes to the fourth stanza, and also helped connect that part of the poem to the earlier image (line 4) of a country "rising from its knees" — an unmistakable reference to a Putin-era slogan. Meanwhile, the Stalinist subtext accounts for the use of the jargon word *gebnyá* (line 17), derived from the Cyrillic initials for "state security." In light of all these signifiers of authoritarian rule, I became a bit worried about the fate of those referenced in the poem's enigmatic ending (which translates literally as "And someone[s] will not return from Capri"). However, Veytsman explained the implication as optimistic — a hint that some people would remain on the island in freedom — so I made a significant edit to the last line as well.

Even after my own research and Veytsman's clarifications, I was still a bit mystified by the third stanza, which introduces characters and images that seem extraneous to both *Buratino* and any possible allegorical parallels: a neighbor woman, a cricket, a rat, and the Hotel Paradiso (of theatrical and cinematic fame). I was tempted to suggest omitting that stanza, but once I took a stab at translating it, I found that it added elements of irreverent levity that impart a gleeful energy to the second half of the poem. Granted, I took several liberties along the way. I "domesticated" the scene of the first line, making substitutions from the nursery rhyme "Three Blind Mice." In the third line, I introduced a vague euphemism for the sake of both delicacy and a poetic assonance I did not want to lose: Veytsman had juxtaposed the words *mukói* (flour) and *mochói* (urine), so I paraphrased the latter as "something fouler" to preserve the phonetic similarity. And I revealed an implicit reference in the fourth line to the circles of Hell (yes, Dante again).

Despite the glaring differences between my wording and the original, Veytsman was delighted with the result. Below is an early draft translation of the entire poem (Veytsman's original and the final English translation can be found on pages 106-107):

AN ITALIAN SKETCH

Draft Translation (Prose)	Final Translation
Having opened the blinds in the living room, you will see the dance of puppets, among whom Papa Carlo, who has rented a modest corner on Capri, is again creating out of cut olive branches a country that has not risen from its knees.	Open the blinds in the living-room — you'll see the puppets clapping a dance round Papa Carlo in his rented digs on Capri where he's been re-creating out of logs from olive trees a country that stays on its knees.
The sun goes down, and the hearth is devoid of ash and letters that smell of anything that pertains to a cat [or] possibly a fox. Meanwhile, nearby there winds a long scarf that costs a single soldo, as though [taken] off the neck of Meyerhold.	The sun goes down, the hearth's swept clean of any ash or letters that might have smelled of cat or fox, the wooden boy's tormentors. But nearby lies a long cheap scarf that could have been unrolled from Puppet-Master Meyerhold.
A neighbor woman walks around with an axe, looking for a cricket and a rat. From the windows [one has] a view of the back entrance of the Hotel Paradiso. It smells of flour, which [smells of] urine, flowing in a parabola above the Nth infernal pile of dregs.	The lady next door hunts for mice, wielding a knife with brio. The windows face the back stairs of the Hotel Paradiso. It smells like flour (or something fouler) sprinkling in the well that leads to Circle X of Hell.

Scrape, chisel! Sing, saw! And shavings, [fly] in various directions to the heights, whirl above the barrel organ to your heart's content and drown out the notes, which will transform into a new anthem to spite the devotees of tranquility, so that there will be something to sing while standing.	Scrape lively, chisel! Sing, old saw! And send your shavings whirling to giddy heights, turning the jingle of the hurdy-gurdy into an anthem for the state enforcers to remand all wanderers to the Motherland.
And this is how a country is obtained — as an alloy of state security tactics and snow. And God will say: "I am the ruler of everything, Alpha and Omega." And there will be darkness, and there will be dreams for each one of God's creatures. And some will not return from Capri.	And this is how a country's forged — from iron fist and frost. And God will say: "I'm Alpha and Omega, I'm the boss." And dark will come, and with it dreams to make God's creatures happy. And some will still run free on Capri.

The examples given in these pages should give some idea of Alexander Veytsman's strengths as a poet — his rich allusiveness, his reverence for Russian poetic tradition, and his technical workmanship — but they alone do not sum up what makes his work unique and worth translating. His poetry occupies a special territory within the genre: Veytsman is an émigré who knows English fluently but still chooses to write in Russian. He is that rare specimen of his generation who has not only learned from the masters of the 19th century (Pushkin, Baratynsky, Tyutchev) and the 20th (Blok, Akhmatova, Pasternak, Mandelshtam) — but has internalized their heritage so deeply that he weaves it seamlessly into scenes of the present day and scenes from his own imagination. Furthermore, he feels a link to the Soviet past that is palpable enough to allow elements of Stalin-era myth, hearsay and legend to permeate his verse like phantoms, both menacing and alluring. The narratives and images that Veytsman presents to the reader are fraught with puzzles, ciphers, mysteries — but the effort of solving them is always worth it. The rewards are a more nuanced understanding of the past, a richer experience of the present, and a soul-stirring encounter with verse that is perceptive, vivid, insightful, elegant. In his unique and resourceful way, Alexander Veytsman draws connections to bygone eras — the ancient world, the European Renaissance, the Russian Empire, the Soviet Union — and bears witness to their historical nightmares and hard-won artistic triumphs. A crucial part of my mission as a translator is to make those connections known to Anglophone readers as well, so that they can hear Veytsman; s poetic testimony for themselves.

In approaching this task over the last several years, I have tried to uphold my overarching principle of poetry translation, which is to convey to the greatest extent possible the creativity, beauty and sensibility that I perceived in the original work. This last phrase is an important caveat: the English works published here represent the aspects of Alexander Veytsman's poems that stand out to *me* as a reader who has an academic background in Russian literature and history. These idiosyncratic points of salience may (or may not) correspond to incidental aspects of my identity: an East Coast Jew with Russian and East European ancestry; an idealist who believes in true love and the indefatigability of human creativity; and an obsessive thinker who loves to discover patterns and solve puzzles. Any of these personality elements has the potential to affect choices in translation, so (as I have told my students many times) an original work can have as many different translations as there are translators.

Mark Polizzotti put it this way in his book *Sympathy for the Traitor*: "A good translation offers not a reproduction of the work but an interpretation, just as the performance of a play or a sonata is a representation of the script or the score, one among many possible representations. I think of it as analogous to a good cover version of a favorite song, one that might not sound like the original but that finds the essence of the song and re-creates it differently; that makes the listener hear the song in a way that both preserves and renews it." (Polizzotti 2019: 53)

Just as with a cover version of modern popular music, part of the attraction and fascination of a translated work is how it differs from the original. Except in the case of a "tribute band," no audience expects a repeat performance of the original, with identical instrumentation, vocal phrasing, harmonies and dynamics; rather, they hope for a new arrangement that has its own musical merit. If the audience knows the original, there is special fascination in comparing the new work against the old: Where are the deviations, what elements have been foregrounded, avoided or invented? For those who do not know the original, a cover version can still be worth a listen if it is well performed and (better still) effectively transmits to the audience what the performer found artistically inspiring in the original. The new rendition might even encourage listeners to seek out the original and learn more about the work of the composer.

If any of the English poems in this collection come across as awkward or obscure, I take full responsibility for these shortcomings, as they are all the result of my own efforts and choices in interpretation, composition or revision. On the other hand, if these translated versions turn out to be aesthetically pleasing, fascinating thought-provoking or inspiring in some way, then that is the result of some element of Alexander Veytsman's genius having been conveyed in translation — and it means my efforts have been worthwhile.

I. УДАЛЯЮЩЕЙСЯ ФИГУРЕ

И задохнулся:
«Анна! Боже мой!»
Давид Самойлов

I. TO A RETREATING FIGURE

And choked through passion:
"Anna! Dear Lord!"
David Samoylov

СЕНТЯБРЬ 2004

Посредством столкновения двух тел
и времени, без прониканья слова,
вначале были ночи и удел
зачатия в двенадцатиметровой
обители, где шторы белокуро
охватывали конус абажура.

Как фон, тогда вибрировал карниз,
пружин тахты глуша стальной избыток.
И было так: благая клетка X
искала сочетанья с клеткой Y.
Ход мыслей, то бушуя, то немея,
озвучивал явление Борея.

Теперь, тот акт спустя — мне двадцать пять.
Я вслушиваюсь в клён, вспотевших окон
касающийся. В стоны, скрип, кровать
за стенкой слева. Снова кто-то создан.
Я вслушиваюсь, зажигаю свечи
и грею воском наступивший вечер.

SEPTEMBER 2004

There came a moment when two bodies met
in time, without a word exchanged by either:
in the beginning was night and the kismet
of life conceived within a twelve-square-meter
apartment, where the blinds reflected blondely
a lampshade's cone, enveloping it fondly.

A curtain rod's vibration joined the swell
as steely strains of couchsprings marked the time.
Here's how it was: a virtuous X cell
was looking for connection with a Y.
A train of thoughts, now muffled, now unbridled,
announced the chilling Boreal wind's arrival.

Now time's moved five-and-twenty years ahead.
I listen to the maple branches grazing
the steamy windows. Moans, a creaking bed
behind the wall. Again, a life created.
I listen, kindle lights, watch the flames weaving,
and with the wax I warm the newborn evening.

ИЗ ГИДА

I

В итоге здесь естественны развалины.
И даже то, что циркулем сравнимо
с проспектами Парижа, в рамках Рима
на скорость разрушения направлено.

Вот Колизей. Вот Форум. Рядом улица,
ведущая к дель Корсо. Дальше — пьяццы:
где можно есть лазанью, обниматься
и думать о руинах. Дальше — слышится

«Счастлив, кто посетил сей мир» из Тютчева,
отчасти проходя за аксиому
и делая прогулку к Пантеону
достойным избежанья делом случая.

II

Холмы. Ступени. Скат наклонной плоскости.
Топографически, на каждой миле
квадратной взгляд терзает изобилье
истории. Политика и подлости.

Мускулатура, шлемы и побоища
до, после варваров. Соски волчицы,
как корм для основателя столицы.
Святейшество, обозванное «овощем»

FROM A GUIDEBOOK

I

Visitors be assured: our ruins are natural.
Even the avenues that laid the graphic
template for Paris to bear its swelling traffic
run headlong toward destruction in our capital.

Don't miss the Colosseum and the Forum.
From there, follow del Corso to piazzas
where tourists can embrace, enjoy lasagna
and think about the ruins. Then the euphoric

"Blessed is he who's visited this world"
that Tyutchev wrote becomes an axiom,
making a stroll to see the Pantheon
a paltry deed that's just as well deferred.

II

Come see the hills, the steps, the landscaped graceful
slopes. Every square mile of this topography
torments the eye with teeming iconography
of history. The decent and disgraceful.

Musculature and helmets. Bloody spectacles,
both pre- and post-barbaric. A view from under
the she-wolf's teats that nursed the city's founder.
His Holiness derided as a "vegetable"

дурными языками. Проявление
пастели Ренессанса. Дом поэта
немецкого. И озирает это
сплав бронзы и величия Аврелия.

III

Всё вперемешку и в пределах города
единого. Когда оставят силы,
в окрестности Треви за ручку с милой
пойди и, заглушая воду шёпотом,

в отверстье ей поведай откровения
ушные. О Барокко. О Вивальди,
Скарлатти. И чуть позже — на кровати
лиши её всего, но не сомнения,

что где-то есть прекрасней география.
И так засни. Морфей сильней Нептуна.
Пусть сон хранит прожитый день подспудно.
Пусть рядом остывают фотографии.

by wicked tongues. The bright emerging genius
of Renaissance pastels. The airy house where
a German poet lived. And gazing outward,
the alloyed bronze and grandeur of Aurelius.

III

You'll find a whole world jumbled in tight quarters
within one city. When your strength is fading,
go take your sweetheart's hand and see the Trevi,
where in a whisper drowning out the water,

into her auricle impart the revelations
you've learned by ear: the great Baroque, Vivaldi,
Scarlatti... Then, in concert with her body,
take everything, and leave no reservations

that any place on earth could suit her more.
Proceed to sleep. Neptune succumbs to Morpheus.
Let dreams preserve this day in your subconscious.
And let the photos curdle in the drawer.

СНЕГ В ОКТЯБРЕ

Александру Рахлину

Он валит примитивно,
как время из песка,
оставив метры ливня
на завтра; а пока

он валит на седины,
на белые кресты,
на сгорбленные спины,
на крики из толпы,

на вырванный из часа
полуденного взгляд:
естественная масса
куда глаза глядят

с небес по вертикали
отправилась затем,
чтоб всюду её ждали,
не только Вифлеем

и Рим, но Массачусетс,
где с пафосом она
воспела эту участь,
сегодня из окна

SNOW IN OCTOBER

To Alexander Rakhlin

It falls like time's old story,
primeval sand through jars;
it might storm down like fury
tomorrow, but so far

it gently falls on gray hairs,
on crosses white as clouds,
on shoulders bent from labors,
on shouts from giddy crowds,

on glances torn of a sudden
from midday colloquy:
a natural abundance
far as the eye can see

sent from the skies to nurture
the hopes of all of them
who wait for some bright future,
not only Bethlehem

and Rome, but Massachusetts,
where ardently it praised
this fortune, whose profuseness
(even with windows raised)

нечёткую для ока,
проснувшегося до
будильника, во сколько
до этого никто

в полукирпичном доме
с колонной не вставал,
сверчка, пожалуй, кроме,
библиотечный зал

который охраняет
у Пруста на виду,
чем временно спасает
и мир, и красоту.

defies the finite power
of eyes that roused before
the alarm rang, at an hour
when no one heretofore

had risen in the brick-and-
mortar colonial,
except perhaps the cricket
that in the library hall

beneath Proust's countenance
fulfills its sentry duty,
thus saving for the nonce
the world and all its beauty.

ГЕФСИМАНСКИЙ САД

Со временем станет ненужною речь,
чей сын я: земной или божий. А станет
естественным эхом опущенный меч
для звуков ударов и звуков стенаний.

Всё меньше тех снов, для которых Отец
собрал эти кости в учительский образ.
Всё реже мне ныне является текст
истории ветхой: теперь он лишь возглас.

Вдыхая пространство живой темноты,
я выжженный куст озираю с тревогой.
Где корни растенья, там корни тщеты
пускаются вглубь, отстраняясь от Бога.

Но новый день будет, и будет он днём,
каких не бывало в минувших столетьях.
Наступит прощенье для всех, а потом
второй день придёт, и он сменится третьим.

THE GARDEN OF GETHSEMANE

Someday there will be no more point in contesting
whose son I am — God's or the earth's. And someday
a sword-beaten-plowshare will be the last vestige
of echoes from slashes and wails of dismay.

The dream-lessons grow ever fewer that Father
assembled these bones in a body to teach.
The testament text for me fades ever farther
in history: now it's just ritual speech.

Inhaling the dark space of living humanity,
I look on the burnt bush with fear in my blood.
Because where its roots are, the long roots of vanity
run deep, growing more and more distant from God.

But a new day will follow, and that day to come
will be for the ages a groundbreaking chapter.
The warmth of forgiveness will touch everyone,
then the next day will dawn, and the third will come after.

РАЗВИВАЯ РЕПЛИКУ

«Я спал, мадонна, видел Ад».
В нём было слишком много света.
Свет излучал спокойный взгляд.
И этот взгляд был взгляд поэта.

— Вергилий, —
                                    я спросил его,
припомнив словеса латыни.
— Я жив иль умер? Кто я? Что
там впереди? Что там отныне?

Учитель! Вождь! Ответь: когда
я сделал то, за что спустился?..
Я умер, да?
                            — Ты умер — да,
ответил мне Вергилий.
                                            — Из-за

неё. Вернее, для неё
ты ныне здесь, вдали от Бога,
с собой неся былое зло
и невозможность диалога.

IN SEARCH OF A REPLY

"Madonna, I just dreamed of Hell."
But it was light like summer days.
That light from a serene gaze fell.
And that gaze was a poet's gaze.

"O Virgil,"
        I called out to him,
recalling words of schoolboy Latin.
"Am I alive or dead? Who am
I? What comes next? And what will happen?

O Teacher! Guide! Pray tell me: Why
did I descend? What was the cause?
I died, right?"
        "Yes, indeed you died,"
Virgil replied to me.
        "Because

of her. Or rather, for her sake
you walk here, far from God's salvation,
bearing your sins without a break
or any chance of conversation."

М. В. ЮДИНА

В Концертном зале у Финляндского вокзала
она сидела на рисунке у поэта.
Возможно, Берга или Бартока играла,
тяжёлым кедом педалируя при этом.
Она сидела в минимальном изложеньи
карандаша и незаметного блокнота.
В застывшем зале при убогом освещеньи
лишь тени рук мешали жанру натюрморта.

Зрачки очками прикрывались так, что зрячесть
могла казаться автономной от Стейнвея.
Все части тела в ней подчёркивали старость.
И даже пальцы шли по клавишам, старея.
Она сидела, и разбитые каноны
пианистической игры валялись подле.
И роль юродивой, согбенной у иконы,
являлась в ней, неискушённой в этой роли.

Она вставала и читала Пастернака.
Закончив, грузно опускала глыбу тела.
И вновь играла. Неподвижным до антракта
был виден профиль с тверди зрительского кресла.
Суровый звук чеканил профиль, как чеканил
тогда всё то, что было в зале. Всё, что было.
А было то, что, в общей массе, христиане
назвали б новым проявленьем Dies Irae.

MARIA YUDINA

To L.D.

Inside the concert hall at Finland Station
she sits in a drawing from a poet's art book.
Her pedaling canvas shoe might be sustaining
the counterpoint of Berg or Bartok.
She sits there, sketched in pencil sparely
against the notebook paper's horizontal bands.
The scene inside the frozen hall, illuminated barely,
would be a still life, if not for the shadows of her hands.

Spectacles hide her pupils, making her perspective
seem trained beyond the Steinway, autonomously ranging.
Every part of her body is stressing the effect of
age. As her fingers touch the keys, even they are aging.
She sits upon the bench as shattered
canons of piano repertory fall beside her.
The feeling of a holy fool, bowed down in rapture
before an icon, bafflingly wells up inside her.

She rises, reads from Pasternak's forbidden compositions,
and sets the boulder of her body down with gravity.
Then goes on playing. Motionless until the intermission
her profile can be seen from the lofty gallery.
The austere sound embosses her, as it embosses
all that the hall contains. Stock still, without a breath.
What's in that hall would make the Christian masses
brace for the blast of the Day of Wrath.

Дух ринулся ввысь, не касаясь перил,
но вскоре рассеялся в облаке страха...
Я вздрогнул от сна и, раскрыв оба века,
на зеркале справа свой взгляд заострил:
в нём мать умирала повторно от рака,
а я отражался наплывом чернил.

Я медленно встал и холодной воды
отпил. Быт привычно просился на ощупь.
Опять доносился Бетховен в звучащих
аккордах. Опять — сквозь уход темноты.
Я вышел из спальни: спокойней и проще
казалось теперь наступленье беды.

* * *

My soul hurtled upward, too giddy to think,
but soon it dispersed in a white cloud of terror...
I jolted awake, and my eyes didn't blink
but stared to the right at the opposite mirror:
my mother was dying of cancer all over
again, while I flailed in a stormwave of ink.

I slowly stood up and threw back a cold glass
of water. By habit, life came to my senses.
Once more I heard Beethoven play in ascending
arpeggios. Once more, as the darkness regressed.
I came out of the bedroom: more simply and gently
the tide of affliction now seemed to flow past.

СТИХИ ИЗ АРХИВА ХУДОЖНИКА

Гляди, Эсхил, как я, рисуя, плачу!
Осип Мандельштам

I. Одалиска

Она лежала полукругом — так лежали
на подушках для Делакруа.
Презрев зрачком неосвещённые детали,
к торсу прикасалась голова.
Сюжет был вырван из кинетики глаголом
эрогенных зон и духоты.
Но дух фантазии меж потолком и полом
проникал в приметы наготы.

На хаос звуков откликалось трио: скрипка,
пианино и виолончель.
В «Анданте» Шуберта, как фон предвечный, зыбко
и тревожно проступала трель.
Журнал «Нью-Йоркер» был раскрыт на узком кресле,
словно некий новый «Арзамас».
И роль сверчка в сей миг присутствовала если,
то скорее в профиль, чем анфас.

Она лежала — абрикосы, сливы, вишни
превращали залу в натюрморт.
Прохлада вымытых волос казалась лишней,
как и по соскам бегущий пот.
Так забывались и обрывки разговоров,
и слова, чьи гласные не счесть,
и ожидание вестей, среди которых
повторилась бы благая весть.

VERSES FROM AN ARTIST'S ARCHIVE

> Look, Aeschylus — as I paint, I cry!
> *Osip Mandelshtam*

I. Odalisque

She lay, her body curved, as models used to pose for
Delacroix, on pillows propped up high.
Her head inclined in nonchalance toward her torso,
unlit details failed to catch her eye.
The subject torn away from palpable kinesis
by erogenous zones and stuffy air,
the stuff of fantasy imbued her naked features,
from the ceiling down to the parterre.

Chaotic ambient sounds were echoed by a trio:
piano, cello, and violin.
Schubert's Andante in the background, played *con brio*,
with a trill gingerly sneaking in.
The New Yorker lay open on a narrow armchair,
like a new edition of Arzamas.
And if a cricket hopped in to play a part there,
it would be in profile, not *en face*.

She lay — beside her, apricots and plums and cherries
made the room a nature morte. The zest
of freshly shampooed hair seemed quite unnecessary,
like the sweat-drops running down her breasts.
The world was all suspended: snatches of conversations,
words blurred in innumerable vowels,
and news deferred by long-forgotten expectations —
even news that might have saved our souls.

II. Инвенция

Двумя руками он нарисовал круг.
Внутри поставил восклицательный знак.
Это был и его лик,
но в первую очередь — Божий.

Он закрыл блокнот и посмотрел на небо.
Ночная иконопись была той же.
Он произнёс по-пастернаковски «Авва
Отче» и дальше забормотал сугубо
личное — для ушей Создателя.

О том, что стало тесно в прежней обители.
О скуке, обживающей разум.
О том, что за исключением птиц,
всё живое общается матом.
Забормотал и, предчувствуя неладное,
пошёл прочь.

II. Invention

With two hands he drew a circle.
Inside he placed an exclamation point.
This was not only his face,
but first and foremost God's.

He closed his notebook and looked at the sky.
The iconic nighttime scene was the same.
He prayed like Pasternak for the cup
to pass, then moved to mutter something purely
personal — for the ears of the Creator:

The place he used to dwell had grown crowded.
Tedium was setting up house in his mind.
With the exception of birds,
all life on earth speaks in obscenities.
He muttered, and sensing impending misfortune,
walked away.

III. Лицо и берег

Писать святых — удел иконописцев.
А я нарисовал тебя.
Такой, какой тебе случиться
пришлось — жеманной, гордой, молчаливой.
И расписался под портретом: «Я,
не заслуживший стать счастливым».

Вдали виднелась синь зрачка и моря,
теснились облака и корабли,
кричали чайки в ре-диез миноре.
Расслабившись, ты жаждала пейзажа,
а я желал портрета лишь.

Но это год спустя уже неважно.

III. Face and Shoreline

The iconographers paint saints with all their passion.
But you were the subject meant for me.
I drew you just the way you happened
to be — genteel and proud, a bit reserved.
And underneath the portrait I signed: "He
for whom a happy life was undeserved."

Your iris matched the sea on the horizon,
the clouds and ships huddled against the blue,
the wheeling seagulls screeched in D# minor.
With limbs relaxed, you craved the landscape distance,
while I preferred the portrait view.

But now a year's gone by, it makes no difference.

МОДИЛЬЯНИ

В те дни Анна Андреевна приходила и раздевалась.
Ложилась на кушетку и таким образом удлинялась.
Представляя собой перешеек света и глины,
мастерская теряла в площади из-за паутины.

Он бредил Египтом, Верленом, сюжетами ада
и рая Данте.
            Огибал углы Люксембургского сада,
да отсчитывал шаги и минуты в сторону Монпарнаса.
Так длился замысел, и пополнялась тара дневного часа.

Ещё не портретист, он уже не признавал пейзажи.
Она задумается над этим позже, заметно старше
став его героев. Старше эль-грекообразных талий
и навеянных кариатидами лицевых деталей.

Они гуляли по городу. И город дробился на лица.
Жизнь казалась медленной, лишённой ярких амбиций.
По походке, по речи, по жестам
                            столетье оставалось
девятнадцатым. И они ощущали радость.

В двадцатом изменится многое:
                            конкретно, проявится смертность.
Смертность придёт, отвлекая,
                        проворно парируя бедность.

MODIGLIANI

Anna Andreyevna would arrive and remove her clothing.
She lay down on the couchette, her long body unfolding.
Extended between light and clay like an isthmus,
encroached on by cobwebs, the studio space diminished.

He raved about Egypt, Verlaine, and tales from the inferno
and paradise of Dante.
          He cut the Luxembourg Garden's corners,
then counted the steps and minutes to Montparnasse.
That's how the plan unfolded and a full day was passed.

Not yet a portraitist, he gave landscapes the cold shoulder.
She would wonder about this later, grown perceptibly older
than his subjects. Older than the El Greco waistlines
and the caryatid-inspired face lines.

They would walk about town. And the town was partitioned
into faces. Life seemed slow, free of flashy ambition.
In its pace, speech and gestures,
          the century remained decided—
ly nineteenth. And they felt delighted.

In the twentieth, much would change:
          specifically, mortality
would arrive, staving off
          and deftly parrying poverty.

Психология города отвергнет ню.

И секс, и Фрейда.

Дадаизм станет главным символом

просвещенья и бреда.

Однако грядущее не столько безумно и бренно,
сколько в контексте минувшего

для взора второстепенно.

Временные процессы Анна Андреевна неплохо
понимала, помечая во взоре уходящую эпоху.

The city's psychology would cast aside nudes.
$$\text{And sex, and Freudian envy.}$$
It would rave about Dada as the symbol
$$\text{of enlightenment and frenzy.}$$

But the future is not merely mad, impetuous or temporary—
in the context of the past,
$$\text{the gaze finds it secondary.}$$
To Anna Andreyevna, these temporal processes grew clearer
as her gaze grimly archived an outgoing era.

МИРО

Лоренсу Богославу

Коллаж. На белом фоне
      треугольники с жёлтым фоном.
Яйцо, приснившееся
          некогда Дали.

Пространство пустоты.
        Жизнь вспять и время оно.
Щепотка пыли.
       Горсть земли.

Свет падает на холст,
      но остаётся посторонним.
Глаз обрамляет свет.

Тьма, сумерки сменив,
      побелена ладонью.
И это новый цвет.

MIRÓ

To Laurence Bogoslaw

Collage. Against the white,
                triangles on a yellow field.
An egg that once was dreamed
                by Dali giving birth.

A space of emptiness.
                Life spun back to days of eld.
A pinch of dust.
                    A fist of earth.

Light falls upon the canvas
                but glances off — still an outsider.
An eye frames light in view.

Darkness eclipses dusk
                but a flat hand rubs it whiter.
And look: that color's new.

* * *

Вот зеркало, в котором были счастливы
с тобой мы зря;
которым плавно создавалось марево
из октября;

которое хранило душу выкреста
и дар прощать;
к которому я припадал в неистовстве
но видел мать.

* * *

Here's the mirror where we watched our happiness
dissolve in vain;
where a fused mirage was gently fashioned from
October rain;

which safeguarded a convert's soul and blessed it by
the gift of grace;
toward which I flew in rage but was arrested by
my mother's face.

НОВОГОДНЕЕ

Проснулся: темень за стеной
играет памятью дневной
и тенью, снова заслонив
мой взгляд на фото тех, кто жив.

Сознание восходит в даль,
в которой часть — горизонталь
тянувшейся руки к руке
на раболепном потолке.

Сознание — за ним слеза
слезу ведёт в бессмертье, за
минувшие часы почти
создав собой объём в горсти.

Проснулся: и дурная весть,
что где-то в этих стенах есть
герой для слога наяву,
как Р. М. Рильке в Беллевю.

NEW YEAR'S

I wake to darkness in the trees
playing on daytime memories
and shadows, once again eclipsing
my view of photos of the living.

Consciousness floats into the dis-
tance, part of whose horizon is
formed by a hand stretched toward a hand
across a servile ceiling spanned.

Consciousness leads tear after tear
rising to the immortal sphere,
swelled through the hours to such a pool
that now my hands are almost full.

I wake up, painfully aware
that deep within these walls somewhere
is a real poet from long ago
like Rilke in his Swiss chateau.

ТРИ ШТУДИИ

(из Бродского)

I. Тридцать два года спустя

На дорогах — ни пробок, ни луж.
Фонари. Ленный холод. Усталость.
Демография дремлющих душ.
Полуночная месса осталась
позади. Средний класс прихожан
видит в праздничных снах Ватикан.

Пред толпой там, пока что горазд
превзойти настоящее время,
Папа Римский сидит, как контраст
новорожденному в Вифлееме.
И толпа, ждя даров, щурит взор:
может, то есть Гаспар? Мельхиор?

Часть религии прячется в снах,
часть — сокрыта в сети Интернета.
В форме ёлки она на глазах.
И, возможно, нет чётче предмета
побудить прихожан и гостей
отойти от морфейских страстей.

На дорогах — ни пробок, ни луж.
Голос прочит осадки на святки.
А за ним — государственный муж
поздравляет солдата в Ираке.
Даст Господь, и с успехом пройдёт
не последний Крестовый поход.

THREE STUDIES
(after Brodsky)

I. Thirty-Two Years After

There's no traffic or mud on the roads.
Lanterns. Weariness. Chill wrapped in flannel.
A succession of somnolent souls.
Midnight mass is long over. The gladful
middle class of parishioners dreams
festive visions of Vatican scenes.

Off in Rome, quite adept at surpassing
the constraints of the present, the pope
sits before the crowd, starkly contrasting
with the babe who gave Bethlehem hope.
The crowd watches for gifts from afar:
"Is that Melchior there? Or Gaspar?"

A religion lives partly in dreams,
and partly on Internet pages.
In its tangible form, evergreens
may be objects far more efficacious
at arousing parishioners and guests
to put passions of Morpheus to rest.

There's no traffic or mud on the roads.
A droll voice predicts snow round the clock.
Then a man of state speaks to the fold
of American troops in Iraq:
May the Lord send His strength to your aid –
best of luck with this latest Crusade.

Красный свет. Под матроску — асфальт.
Слева — берег квадратного пруда.
Бомж с бомжихой бесцельно глядят,
как Иосиф с Марией до чуда.
Сын родился, и сдвинулась ось.
Бытие Рождества началось.

24 декабря 2003

A small pond to the left of a square.
A red light. A sailor-striped crosswalk.
A street couple aimlessly stare
like pre-miracle Mary and Joseph.
A son's born; the earth shifts as it spins.
So the Season of Christmas begins.

December 24, 2003

II. Дидоне

Я покидаю не тебя, а Карфаген.
Не настоящее, а будущее время.
И это не удел и не судьба,
А следствие естественного ветра.
Есть вещи в этой жизни, для которых
Мы созданы без права удивляться.
Возможно, что без права вообще.

Оглядываясь на заснувший город,
Не вижу я ни призраков, ни зла.
Небытие — оно и пережито,
И, между тем, пока не наступило.
Разноголосица преследует зарю.
То море, вдоль которого мы прежде
Гуляли, постепенно исчезает.

Я не вернусь, поскольку в никуда
Возможно возвратиться только вместе.

Столетие закончится. Вода
Остынет. На холмах осядет почва.
Лицо скрывая в локоны, пророк
Вздохнёт и пожалеет о речённом.
Но тоже не вернётся в Карфаген.

II. To Dido

It isn't you I'm leaving — it's the shores of Carthage.
It's not the present time I'm leaving, it's the future.
And this is not my luck and not my fate —
It's just a consequence of nature's wind.
There are some things in this life for which
We're made, without the right to be surprised.
And maybe without any right at all.

As I look backward at the sleeping city,
I see no phantom shades, I see no evil.
Oblivion is something we've lived through,
And at the same time, hasn't yet occurred.
Dissonance chases off the light of dawn.
The sea alongside which we used to
Take walks is slowly disappearing.

I won't return, for nowhere is a place
We can't return unless we are together.

The century will end. The water
Will cool. Upon the hills the soil will sink.
Hiding his face in his long locks, the prophet
Will sigh and feel regret for what was spoken.
And yet he, too, will not return to Carthage.

III. Январская элегия

Анатолию Розенцвейгу

...а странное было таковым:
плафоны из зелёных превращались в красные,
в такт приходящему «ты» из уходящего «вы»
русской диаспоры,
к тому времени вдохнувшей ровно сорок
градусов кориандровой, вишнёвой,
незаметной, как полигоны корок
чёрных и жизни новой.

...а тень, не имевшая учеников
при жизни, бродила среди апостолов
и в евангелие из рифмованных слов
вслушивалась —
бродила вокруг да около
пиджаков и платьев, из моды
не вышедших лишь по причинам лени
и накопивших монотонные годы,
чтобы ниже поклониться тени.

...а со стены смотрел тоскующий взгляд
волчицы, представляющей лукавого
с тех первых дней двенадцать лет назад,
когда обитателей дантовых
стало на единицу больше, когда в мире
стало на единицу меньше,
когда исчезло время
для сосков, которые не вскормили
ни Ромула, ни Рема.

III. January Elegy

To Anatoly Rosenzweig

...and the strange thing was this:
the lights overhead changing from green to red
in time with the incoming *ty* replacing the outgoing *vy*
of the Russian diaspora, which by then
had ingested a good hundred
degrees of coriander, cherry,
unremarkable as polygons of humdrum
black bread, and new life in the belly.

...and the shadow that had no one to teach
while alive now roamed among the apostles
and listened intently
to the rhyming speech
of what they called their gospels —
roaming around the suits and dresses that hadn't gone
out of fashion because it was just too much bother
and had taken years of monotony on
so they could bow down to the shadow lower.

...and from the wall came a longing glow
from the gaze of the wolf that has symbolized the evil
one since those early days twelve years ago
when the population of Dante's medieval
work became one greater, and that of the world
became one less,
when time became heedless
of the teats that had fed
neither Romulus nor Remus.

БОСТОНСКИЕ РИФМЫ

1

Я люблю тебя таким, каким задумал Бог.
Я пишу в надежде написать не эпилог.
Жизнь не вписывается при всех стараньях в мозг.

2

Паутина украшает прежний
                              интерьер.
Чтобы слушать Шумана, мы тянемся в партер.
Суховатым кажется Бердяев. И Вольтер.

3

Глаз привычно остывает. Остывает чай.
Вспоминаешь выборочно what escapes the eye.
....

4

Абажур бледнеет. По стене ползёт пыльца.
В раме застревает полевая стрекоза.
До восхода солнца остаётся три часа.

BOSTON RHYMES

1

I love you just the way that God intended you to be.
As I write, I hope this tale will go on endlessly.
Life can't fit inside my brain — it's just too tight a squeeze.

2

Spiderwebs festoon the rooms that once were decked
          with flair.
Strains of Schumann's music draw us out on the parterre.
Old Berdyaev seems a little dry. So does Voltaire.

3

Tea turns cold. A glance turns cold. And no one wonders why.
We selectively remember what escapes the eye.
....

4

Light subdues the lampshade. Dust mites drift along the wall.
There's a dragonfly aflutter in the window well.
Three more hours left until the sunrise tops the hill.

5

Некому воскликнуть ныне про «товарищ, верь!»
Раздаётся скрип окна, но нет — то только дверь.
Шум, несущий март и какофонию потерь.

6

Для демографа мы вместе прошагали треть.
....
Вырваться из общей массы я сочту за честь.

7

Будущее исчезает под приставкой «лже».
После нас останутся тетради и клише.
Справедливо, что о нас не вспомнят вообще.

8

Чем смиренней кашель,
                            тем прохладнее висок.
....
Мысли чёрные придут.
                            Придут наискосок.

9

Вопреки гармонии стремишься жизнь менять.
Дольник неподатливый хореем упрощать.
В той, что раздевал вчера, искать сегодня блядь.

5

There's nobody left to shout "Our star will rise once more!"
I can hear a window creak — but no, it's just a door.
March brings a cacophony of losses to endure.

6

Demographic experts say our path is one-third trod.
....
I'd feel honored in the end to break free from the crowd.

7

Lost in one big "pseudo-" our whole future fades away.
What we leave behind will be just notebooks and clichés.
Just as well that we won't be remembered anyway.

8

As your cough grows more subdued,
                              the cooler your head feels.
....
Black thoughts will be coming.
                    They'll come on each other's heels.

9

You'll disrupt your well-tuned lifestyle just to be perverse.
Simplify the jagged dolniks to trochaic verse.
Call the one you undressed yesterday a whore, or worse.

10

Мне привычен клюв белоголового орла.
Для двуглавого я — тень забытого посла.
Скоро буду жечь бумаги и сдавать дела.

11

Герметизм не позволяет вздёрнуть жалюзи.
....
Горизонт сокрыт вуалью облака в грязи.

12

Где-то бродит по аллеям абсолютный слух.
Мощь тротила глушится назойливостью мух.
Мухобойки глушат звон семейных оплеух.

13

Кто есть лишний? Кто есть нужный? Кто есть тот герой?
....
....

14

В белом венчике из роз — вдали Исус Христос.
Память и прощение батрачат на износ.
Разум тихо внемлет гулу половых желёз.

10

I've grown used to this bald eagle as a longtime host.
To the double-headed one, I'm just an envoy's ghost.
Soon I'll burn my documents and then resign my post.

11

Hermetism doesn't let you raise the jalousies.
....
Horizontal clouds of dust lay veils upon the trees..

12

Perfect pitch is roving where the tree-lined pathway lies.
Blasts of dynamite are drowned out by the buzz of flies.
Flyswatters drown out the din of family hues and cries.

13

Who's superfluous? Who's needed? Who's the hero now?
....
....

14

In a white wreath made of roses, Jesus walks alone.
Memory and forgiveness work their fingers to the bone.
Reason meekly hearkens to the low gonadic drone.

ИЗ ЭЙЗЕНШТЕЙНА

Вите Лещинской

1

Вода безумна, как танец опричников.
Течёт и сужается в городах издавна.
Несёт тела, не хороня их,
и неясно, что хоронит именно.

2

То холод взывает к потусторонней помощи,
то слышится Ледовое побоище,
то дуновение со свистом
становится дуновением ноющим.

3

Покинув воду и вообразив лестницу,
немало, верно, иному померещится,
помешанному на единице,
на которую ничего не делится.

SCENES FROM EISENSTEIN

To Vita Leshinsky

1

Water is wild, like the dance of the oprichniks.
It flows through towns, widening and shrinking.
It carries bodies without burying them.
And what it does bury just keeps on sinking.

2

It may call upon cold for otherworldly assistance,
the Battle on the Ice may clash in the distance,
or the wind may turn from a whistle
to a wind whining with pathetic insistence.

3

Leaving the water, a spirally winding
walkway upward must seem quite inviting
to someone obsessed with a unit
by which nothing can be divided.

Прислушайтесь: из пыльного угла,
где некогда висели зеркала,
доносится холодный и невнятный
звук голоса, летящий к небесам, —
и это сочиняет Мандельштам
стихи про неизвестного солдата.

Прислушайтесь: послышится «Аминь»,
как признак жизни там, где раньше жизнь
теплилась, наделённая глухими
и ветхими молитвами, жизнь та,
что начинает с имени Христа,
а завершается, совсем не помня имя.

Прислуш... опять идёт январский снег,
рифмуя прежним ямбом новый век,
что кажется логичным, ибо ямбы
одёргивают время — шаг, вздох, взгляд —
и в прошлое торжественно спешат,
чтоб лечь под светом керосинной лампы.

* * *

Sssh! Listen closely — in a dusty nook
where once a mirror hung upon a hook,
you'll make out, muttering coldly from the corner,
a voice ascending to the sky:
it's Mandelshtam composing on the fly
his verses in the unknown soldier's honor.

Sssh! Listen — and you'll hear the word "Amen":
the phantom of a life that lived within
an envelope of warmth endowed with softened
time-honored Pentateuchal prayers — a life
beginning with the name of Christ
and ending with the name now quite forgotten.

Sssh... January snow rings in new time,
but marks it with an old iambic rhyme —
which stands to reason, for iambic feet
hold fast the time — a step, a sigh, a glance —
and march triumphantly into the past
to rest beneath a lamp's light and heat.

МОСКОВСКИЕ ОТРЫВКИ

I

Так заканчивается май.
Тревога, судорога в шее.
Внезапный холод батареи.
Обрывок дня. «Прощай!» —
в обрывке фразы. Голоса
Электры и Ореста.
Лишь демону известно,
что будет через два часа.

Так заканчивается май.
На подоконнике цветок и кактус.
На LCD — похоже, «Казус
Кукоцкого». Чернеет чай
и не дымится. Здесь экран,
как будто штора; моль же —
как будто муха. Боже:
в окне — лицо, за ним — каштан.

Так заканчивается май.
Так — приближеньем рака.
Отдельной смертью Пастернака.
Когда «Прошу, не догорай», —
судьба опять твердит свече,

MOSCOW EXCERPTS

I

Here's how the end of May goes by.
A cramp in the neck, an anxious quaver.
The sudden chill of a radiator.
The snatch of a day. "Good-bye!"
in the snatch of a phrase. Voices grow louder:
Orestes and Electra.
Only a daemon could predict what
may happen in the next two hours.

Here's how the end of May goes by.
A flower and a cactus by the window.
A TV show dissects the riddle
of Dr. Kukotsky. Russian chai
turns black, with no more steam. The screen
flits like a blind; a tiny
moth flits like a fly. Almighty
God: there's a face in front of the chestnut tree!

Here's how the end of May goes by.
With cancer's footsteps at our backs.
Recalling the death of Pasternak.
"Please, don't burn out!" — the battle cry
raised to the candleflame by fate.

а на востоке вместо
лучей восходит резко
меняющееся в лице.

II

В этот вечер портрет заменён фотографией,
«Баядерка» — «Жизелью»,
стих в альбом — эпитафией.

В этот вечер сто ватт нагорают на семьдесят,
зеркалам не до трещин,
тень за светом не следует.

В этот вечер дневник встретил прозу терцинами,
прежним ямбом из Данте
и другой половиною.

III

Да, возможно и так. Но, как прежде,
остаются все темы, хоть без
вариаций. Так будет до смерти,
продолжающей данный процесс
бытия при потушенном свете
и тускнеющем смысле небес.

And in the east instead of
sunbeams a glaring spread of
expressions shifting on that face.

II

This evening a portrait's replaced with a photograph,
Bayadère with Giselle,
an album verse with an epitaph.

This evening a hundred watts burn down to seventy,
mirrors don't care to crack,
light and shadow fall separately.

This evening my diary sets prose lines in ternaries,
meeting Dante halfway
through the rest of eternity.

III

Yes, it could be that way. But the thing is,
all the themes stay the same, just without
variations. And so it continues
until death, which will play the piece out
with the light of existence extinguished
and the meaning of heaven in doubt.

IV

И всё же,
как рефрен, —
прости меня,
прости
за то, что я —
не ты,
а ты —
лишь вымысел.
За то,
что речь есть дар,
а Бог недаром
не дал,
а выбросил.

IV

Again,
like a refrain:
forgive me, please
forgive
the fact
that I'm not you,
and you
are just a fiction.
That yes,
speech is a gift,
but one God didn't give,
but cast
off like an affliction.

УДАЛЯЮЩЕЙСЯ ФИГУРЕ

Она не бледна, как смерть. Она и есть
                                    смерть.
Всегда была и, естественно, есть.

Она сбрасывает шаль, вполоборота застыв
вначале на холсте, а затем — как миф.

Она приходит с косой, а уходит с тобой,
заглушая твой голос русской землёй.

Она есть ты. Она — твой словарь,
который пора менять,
                        как и дверной фонарь.

TO A RETREATING FIGURE

She's not as pale as death. She is
                                  death.
Has always been and, naturally, still is.

She casts off her shawl, and in mid-turn goes stiff
in brushstrokes on canvas, then morphs into myth.

She arrives with a scythe, and leaves with your life,
stills your voice with the Russian earth holding you tight.

She is you. She's your whole lexicon,
which now must be changed
                          like a porchlight that won't go on.

II. ВДОЛЬ ПОБЕРЕЖЬЯ

И взблескивала серая вода,
Поскольку тень туда не доставала.
Дмитрий Быков

II. ALONG
THE COAST

And the gray water shimmered in the light,
Because it was beyond the reach of shadow.
Dmitry Bykov

ВДОЛЬ ПОБЕРЕЖЬЯ

Биане

Дорога не заканчивается,
    и не заканчивается Массачусетс.
Впереди вереница
    успевших проснуться улиц.
Пуритане встают,
    как правило, перед рассветом.
Особенно теперь,
    когда лето.

Проснись, подруга,
    и в лёгком до-миноре
пропой мелодию
    новым краям и морю,
захватившему силой
    весь левый берег взгляда.
Проснись,
    и пускай прохлада

ворвётся в оконную щель
    со скоростью километров
в сто двадцать — сто тридцать.
    Пускай незатейливым ветром
продуваются мысли,
    летящие за борт
и на северо-запад.

ALONG THE COAST

To Biana

There's no end to the road,
    and no end to Massachusetts.
Up ahead file neat rows of streets
    that awoke with the roosters.
These Puritans tend to rise
    before dawn from their slumbers.
Especially now
    that it's summer.

Wake up, girlfriend,
    and sing me a nice easy C-
minor melody heralding
    new frontiers and the sea,
which has taken by force
    the entire left bank of our vision.
Let the cool air
    come swishing

through the crack of the window
    at speeds of a hundred and twenty
or thirty kilometers.
    Let the wind, laid-back and friendly,
blow away all the thoughts
    that are seeking release
toward the northeast.

BATTERY PARK CITY

Вода, вода, как страх и прах, — везде.
Душа уходит в пятки, взгляд — к звезде.
И месяц освещает тьму ладони.

По набережной бродит Гумилёв,
ход дум добавив к ходу облаков,
а шёпот — к тишине потусторонней.

И под, и над, и вне, окрест — вода.
Немного волн. Немного рыб. Немного льда.
Гармония закончится дуэлью.

И Гумилёв, отстукивая шаг,
как будто ямб, воображает, как
жмёт руку гражданину Коктебеля.

И он её пожмёт, когда вдали
появится рассвет, и громко «пли!»
воскликнет молодой красноармеец.

Затем бесшумно вырвется «Аминь!»
Затем исчезнет всё, включая жизнь.
И соскользнёт с ладони влажный месяц.

BATTERY PARK CITY

Water, water everywhere — like fright and night.
Your soul leaps back — a star leaps into sight.
The moon lights up the shadows in your palm.

There's Gumilyov — along the bank he broods,
adding his train of thought to the train of clouds,
his whisper to the otherworldly calm.

Water — above, below, around, all sides.
Some lapping waves. Some fish. Some floating ice.
A duel is about to break the tranquil spell.

And Gumilyov, measuring off his steps
like iambs, in his imagination grips
the hand of a gentleman from Koktebel.

His grip will tighten as the distant sun
peeks over the horizon and a young
Red Army soldier barks the order: "Fire!"

Then noiselessly the triggered word "Amen!"
Then everything, including life, will end.
And from your palm the moonlight will expire.

* * *

Д. С.

В этот день, распрощавшись с семьёй,
   он сказал, что теперь
он уходит в ту даль,
   где река не граничит с туманом,
а глаза не краснеют
   в предчувствии новых потерь,
сочинённых по ходу зимы
   повзрослевшим тираном.

«Облака», — он сказал
   и пошёл с рюкзаком на спине,
не оглядываясь на соседей,
   стоявших поодаль,
напевая лесную мелодию —
   ту, что во сне
он услышал намедни
   и тотчас связал со свободой.

«Облака», — повторили соседи,
   вернувшись домой,
где достали из шкафа одежду
   в небрежных заплатах,
что давно прекратила питать
   постаревшую моль,
но не вышла из моды
   для красок речного заката.

* * *

To D. S.

When he bade his farewells to his family,
    he said he was off
to the place where the river blends in
    with the mist in the distance
where one's eyes don't turn red
    at the thought of a winter of loss
at the hands of a tyrant just grown
    out of cruel adolescence.

"Oh the clouds..." he intoned
    as he shouldered his pack and set forth
past the bystanding neighbors
    as though he did not even see them,
and he whistled a wild sylvan tune
    he had heard once before
in a dream and divined straightaway
    as a portent of freedom.

"Oh the clouds..." said the neighbors
    in turn as they headed back home
where they took out their crudely
    patched clothing from deep in their closets
which the moths had stopped feeding
    on long ago since they were grown
but still matched the perennial colors
    of riverside sunsets.

* * *

Ты помнишь школу — так, чтоб вдалеке,
в тьме гладиолусов и красках паутины
включили свет, рассеянный в тоске,
и видеть три портрета, три картины:
Надежды Ф., Елены А. и Нины
Владимировны с рупором в руке?

Ты помнишь тот дверной проём? За ним
виднелась лестница, за ней виднелась осень.
Казалось: вот пройдёт — и полетим
туда, где не поют про двадцать восемь
героев, где, завидев неба просинь,
не рвутся ввысь под михалковский гимн.

Ты помнишь, как прошли все тридцать лет?
И что случилось в школе номер 30?
(Возможно, дело в прочерках). Я — нет.
Возможно, скоро снова повторится
жизнь в гладиолусах, разбитая на лица,
лишь в новой паутине будет свет.

* * *

Do you remember our old school — through strands
of darkened gladioli and colored cobwebs screening
in light that got switched on from neverland —
and see three portraits with composed demeanor:
Nadezhda F., Yelena A. and Nina
Vladimirovna with megaphone in hand?

Do you remember that doorway? Peeking through
we saw a stairway, and beyond that — autumn.
It seemed like once it passed, we'd fly off to
someplace where no one sings of twenty-eight awesome
heroes, or jumps up for the Soviet anthem
whenever they happen to see the sky turn blue.

Do you remember how thirty years have passed?
And all that happened in School Number 30?
I don't. (Perhaps the records are erased.)
Perhaps some life will once again be bursting
with gladioli, faces seen transversely
through light that breaks upon new cobwebs' lace.

* * *

Улисс вернулся домой,
   а дома опять ни души.
На небе — ни сини, ни облака.
   Говорят, горизонт в глуши
спешит за отсутствием света,
   и этим бросает фортуне
существенный вызов в апреле,
   но чаще всего в июне.

Улисс спешит по соседям
   и тихо бормочет: «Когда
меня покинет память
   и, значит, покинет беда?»
Соседи его не слышат,
   но, видя диковинный профиль,
кричат о победе в мае,
   как будто о катастрофе.

Улисс затем подумал:
   «Кем выдумана та западня,
что миру дала Лаэрта,
   а Лаэрту дала меня?»
И понял, что будет жить дальше,
   теперь, впрочем, не объясняя
себе совсем ничего,
   помимо собачьего лая.

* * *

Ulysses returned to his home,
    but at home there was nary a soul.
The sky was not cloudy or blue.
    The hinterland horizon, some hold,
impetuously races toward darkness,
    thus posing an inopportune
challenge to fortune in April,
    but even more often in June.

Ulysses runs from neighbor to neighbor,
    muttering quietly: "When
will memory leave me for good,
    and thus ill fortune leave me again?"
The neighbors don't hear him,
    but seeing his outlandish profile
they shout about victory in May,
    as though it were something quite awful.

Ulysses was struck by a thought:
    "Who thought up that cruel irony
that gave the world Laertes,
    and gave Laertes me?"
And he realized that he'd keep on living,
    but would no longer have to explain
to himself anything at all
    but an old dog's barking refrain.

RUE DE RENNES

Бледный Бунин заметил, как камень с моста
покатился на площадь, и площадь пуста
стала, словно приставили зеркало к небу.
Был ли это сам Бунин? А может быть, не был?

Как бы ни было, все говорили, что был.
Силуэт, запах шляпы, пятно от чернил
в том парижском кафе намекали на чудо:
будто вновь он пришёл, будто будет, покуда

в Сен-Сюльпис не закончится воск, а сыры
не покроются плесенью — эти миры
изобрёл не он сам, а, напротив, Арсеньев,
и, скорей, не миры, а их скромные тени.

Бледный Бунин заметил, как камень... — и да,
камень вправду катился и был навсегда
связан с днём, когда люди и дикие звери,
обнимая друг друга, шептались в неверьи.

Ибо призрак есть призрак. В попытке взглянуть
на него в этот день наступивший был путь
к пониманию памяти, что в рамках страха
о подножье моста бьётся пеплом под Баха.

RUE DE RENNES

Bunin blanched by the bridge when he saw a stone roll
off the edge and bounce onto the square, then the whole
square cleared out like a mirror held up to the heavens.
Had that been the real Bunin? Or maybe it hadn't?

Let that be as it may, they all said it had been.
A black outline, a hat, an inkblot from a pen
in that Paris café... these were signs bona fide
that he'd been back again, and that he would abide

until Saint Sulpice ran out of wax, and the cheese
all grew moldy — these worlds were not his
to invent, but Arsenyev's (or Dersu Uzala's)
and they weren't worlds, but shadows in muted gray colors.

Bunin blanched by the bridge when he saw... and in fact,
the stone really did roll and would always roll back
to the day when wild beasts and forebears of our race
had whispered in disbelief as they embraced.

For a ghost is a ghost. Those who tried on that day
to catch sight of it might have discovered a way
we can understand memory, beating back fear
and our ancestors' ashes as Bach fills our ears.

ИЗ ТАРКОВСКОГО

Александру Друяну

Загляни в этом дом,
    где на нотах с ноктюрном пыльца
отделяет бемоль
    от тумана сентябрьским рассветом,
а затем исчезает за тенью,
    овала лица
не касаясь совсем,
    и не слыша уже: «Вот и лето...

Вот и лето прошло!» —
    не осталось, считай, никого,
кто бы смог прочитать
    эти строки с намёком на шёпот;
загляни в этот дом,
    где в надежде пролить молоко
пианист задевает стакан
    и не слышит потопа

за окном, что продолжится
    после шестого числа
двое суток подряд,
    а потом поутихнет к восьмому,
чтобы кто-то сказал en passant:
    «Вот и осень прошла!» —
загляни в этот дом,
    но останься неведомым дому.

AFTER TARKOVSKY

To Alexander Druyan

Take a peek in that house,
   where the pollen is playing on notes
of a nocturne and sifting
   the flats through the dawn of September
before ducking in back of a shadow,
   not lighting at all
on the curve of a face
   and not hearing the words "Now the summer...

Now the summer is gone!"
   And there's no one left—look!—not a soul
who could read these lines even in whispertones,
   much less out loud;
take a peek in that house,
   where the hope of spilt milk is compelling
a pianist to elbow a glass
   without hearing the swelling

of the flood at the window outside,
   which will keep pressing on
till the sixth of the month cascades
   into the eighth, not subsiding
until someone remarks *en passant*:
   "Now the autumn is gone!"
Take a peek in that house,
   but don't let the house know where you're hiding.

ИТАЛЬЯНСКАЯ ЗАРИСОВКА

Алану и Амели

Раскрыв в гостиной жалюзи,
    увидишь танец кукол,
среди которых папа Карло,
    снявший скромный угол
на Капри, снова создаёт
    из колотых поленьев
страну, не вставшую с коленей.

Заходит солнце, и камин
    лишён золы и писем,
кошачьим чем-то пахнувших,
    возможно, чем-то лисьим.
А рядом вьётся длинный шарф
    ценой в единый сольдо,
как будто с шеи Мейерхольда.

Соседка ходит с топором,
    ища сверчка и крысу.
Из окон — вид на чёрный вход
    отеля Парадисо.
Мукою пахнет, что мочой,
    параболой текущей
над N-ной инфернальной гущей.

Строгай, рубанок! Пой, пила!
    И стружки — врозь к высотам,
кружитесь над шарманкой всласть
    и заглушайте ноты,

AN ITALIAN SKETCH

To Alan and Amelie

Open the blinds in the living-room—
    you'll see the puppets clapping
a dance round Papa Carlo
    in his rented digs on Capri
where he's been re-creating
    out of logs from olive trees
a country that stays on its knees.

The sun goes down, the hearth's swept clean
    of any ash or letters
that might have smelled of cat or fox,
    the wandering boy's tormentors.
But nearby lies a long cheap scarf
    that could have been unrolled
from Puppet-Master Meyerhold.

The lady next door hunts for mice,
    wielding an axe with brio.
The windows face the back stairs
    of the Hotel Paradiso.
It smells like flour (or something fouler)
    sprinkling in the well
that leads to Circle X of Hell.

Scrape lively, chisel! Sing, old saw!
    And send your shavings whirling
to giddy heights, turning the jingle
    of the hurdy-gurdy

что превратятся в новый гимн
назло жрецам покоя,
чтоб было что петь стоя.

И так получится страна —
как сплав гэбни и снега.
И скажет Бог: «Я – Вседержитель,
Альфа и Омега».
И будет тьма, и будут сны
для каждой божьей твари.
И кто-то не вернётся с Капри.

into an anthem for the state
    enforcers to remand
all wanderers to the Motherland.

And this is how a country's made —
    from iron fist and frost.
And Alpha-God will say: "I am your King,
    the first and last."
And dark will come, and with it dreams
    to make God's creatures happy.
And some will still run free on Capri.

ЛЕТО, ВЗЯТОЕ В СКОБКИ

(Я посмотрел в стекло: внутри потел июль,
молчанием зазывая ми-бемоль
мажор из ноктюрна Шопена).

Не обращая внимания на стекло и пот,
прохожие шли мимо и виноград
прожёвывали монотонно.

Стекло казалось то зеркалом, то стеной,
готовой загородить царство теней
от будничного царства.
В стекле отражалось другое стекло,
а в мёртвом Гудзоне — удар весла
о приближающийся остров.

Июль восхищался даром реки
безмолвно объединять облака
в простые, ливневые причуды.
Осадки заканчивались раньше, чем
могли закончиться в любом ином
месяце юлианского года.

Молчание, вести навстречу летя,
вначале — рядом, чуть позже — везде
и тоталитарно наступало.
Сливаясь со скукой, молчание вскользь
по набережной двигалось и вес
времени сбрасывало то и дело.

A SUMMER IN PARENTHESES

(I looked into a pane of glass: inside July was steaming,
the silence conjuring E-flat
major from a nocturne by Chopin.)

Paying no mind to the glass or steam,
pedestrians walked by with grapes
monotonously chewing.

The glass by turns a mirror and a wall
ready to fence off the realm of shadows
from the realm of everyday.
Reflected in the glass was another glass,
and in the limpid Hudson — the stroke of an oar
against an approaching island.

July admiring the river's gift
of wordlessly uniting clouds
into simple, torrential wonders.
Spates of rain ending sooner than
they could have ended in any other
month of the Julian calendar.

Silence, flying to greet new tidings,
at first nearby — a beat later, everywhere
taking totalitarian hold.
Blending with longing, a slipstream of silence
moving along the embankment, the weight
of time sloughing off along the way.

Ноктюрн вослед начинал звучать,
и на горизонте начиналась ночь,
из сумерек тесных возникая.
Арпеджио следовали ровно по
воде, а за ними спешила толпа
нот, сыгранных правой рукою.

The nocturne in its wake beginning to play
and on the horizon night beginning,
arising from thickly settled dusk.
Arpeggios rowing evenly upon
the water... then after them came a throng
of notes played with a trebling hand.

В***

Она могла б сыграть Ахматову.
Седую, грузную, высокую.
А здесь — Чечня.
Окрест — Чечня.
Война, лишённая войны и мира.
Её приходится на веру принимать.
Как духоту.

В ней кроется действительно Ахматова.
Не столько ум и стан — самодержавие.
В ней кроется ещё знакомый голос.
А здесь —
Не слух, а лишь попытка слышать речь.
Запас двусложных слов…
И душно.

V***

She could have played Akhmatova.
White hair, her heavy build, her stately height.
But this is Chechnya.
The midst of Chechnya.
A war that's neither war nor peace.
It has to be accepted on faith.
Like the stifling heat.

She really has Akhmatova inside her.
Not just her mind and figure, but her self-determination.
Also inside her is a familiar voice.
But here–
She doesn't speak, just tries to hear what's said.
A stack of two-syllable words stored up...
And stifled.

МОНОЛОГ КАВАФИСА

Прости мне, Господи, попытку слышать речь.
И речь саму прости.
Я сжёг бы рукопись, коль можно было б сжечь,
чтоб прах в горсти
был продолжением твоим

                   в моей мольбе.
Хвала тебе!

Прости мне, Господи, что не путём зерна
движение строки
уходит вглубь, касаясь фрейдовского сна,
что вопреки
тому, что рифма у рассудка отняла,
звучит хвала!

Прости мне, Господи, мужской запретный плод,
размеренно в кафе
напротив пьющий ароматный кислород,
бросая две
монеты юноше, чей образ золотой
есть образ твой.

Прости и то, что осквернённая вода
на землю пролилась
и что, где прежде я не оставлял следа,
гноится грязь.
Прости за то, что я вхожу в Ерусалим,
но вижу Рим.

CAVAFY'S MONOLOGUE

Forgive me, Lord, for trying to hear thy words.
And please forgive mine own.
I would have burned the manuscript if only it could burn
yet still live on
as ash between my palms that would prolong
                                thee in my prayers.

I sing thy praise!

Forgive me that the self-effacing way of grain
is not the way my line
runs deep into the Freudian furrows of my brain
and that despite
what rhyme has stripped from reason, what remains
still sings thy praise!

Forgive me, Lord, the sight across the way
of male forbidden fruit
drinking aromatic oxygen in a cafe
and tossing two
coins to a youth whose image, bronzed and fine,
is made in thine.

Forgive me, too, the desecrated water poured
upon the earth's pure face
and please forgive the filth that festers where before
I'd left no trace.
Forgive me that into Jerusalem I come,
but I see Rome.

ОСЕНЬ 2008

Финансовый кризис продолжается, и берег Гудзона
становится холоднее.
Я прогуливаюсь в чёрном пальто,
взглядом обрусевшего еврея
встречая шагающих мимо хасидов.
Такие бороды носили лет сто
назад в местах, где потом побывали немцы.
Ветер вздыхает монотонно,
колыша лодками и не торопясь к сердцу.
Недорогое сукно, как элемент быта
и бюджета, покрывается солью капель.
Цена нефти за баррель
тем временем падает изо дня в день.

Это дивная новая экономика,
чья некогда невидимая рука
отрублена, словно по шариату.
Память о ней тянется от заката
к закату, целомудренное облако
развращая до фривольных осадков.
Идёт дождь. Денег нет. Адам Смит умер.
Безмолвствует река.
И едва заметное утро
виднеется издалека.

Утро есть пробуждение. Ты откроешь глаза
и машинально полезешь ими на потолок.
Раздастся лай кастрированного пса.

FALL 2008

The financial crisis continues, and the bank of the Hudson
becomes colder.
I stroll around in a black coat,
with the gaze of a Russified Jew
meeting the Chasids striding past.
Such beards were worn a hundred or so years
ago in towns later occupied by Germans.
The wind sighs monotonously,
rocking the boats but not rushing to the heart.
Inexpensive cloth, like a slice of life
and the budget, is covered with the salt of drops.
The price of oil per barrel
meanwhile falls from day to day.

This is the wondrous new economy,
whose once invisible hand
has been lopped off, like under Sharia law.
The memory of it lingers from sunset
to sunset, the chaste cloud
corrupting/depraving/perverting to frivolous precipitation.
It's raining. There's no money. Adam Smith is dead.
The river is silent.
And a barely perceptible morning
comes into view from far away.

Morning is an awakening. You open your eyes
and mechanically climb them up to the ceiling.
You'll hear the bark of a castrated dog.

Шопен ворвётся продолжительной трелью,
прерывая продолжительный вздох.
Слух застигнет врасплох
очередная финансовая весть.
И губы, что ни разу ещё не холодели,
начнут холодеть.

Chopin will leap in in a prolonged trill,
interrupting a prolonged sigh.
The ear will be caught unawares by
the latest financial news.
And lips that never once got chilled before
will start chilling.

ЕДВА ЛИ РОМАНС

Биане

Пришла метель, пришла благодаря
тому, что всплыло на кофейной гуще.
Пришла и перестала быть грядущей.
И год закончился двадцатым декабря.

Сняла пальто, за ним — бордовый шарф,
сняла перчатки, бросив шаль к камину.
Пришла, и оказалось, что с повинной,
губами медленно к руке его припав.

Едва она припала, прежний взгляд
лишился памяти и превратился в четверть
шестого, чтобы напоследок встретить
восход, напоминающий закат.

А новым взглядом был не взгляд, а путь
её двух глаз в его два спящих глаза,
который был однажды ей предсказан
как побеждающий бессонницу и грусть.

HARDLY A ROMANCE

To Biana

There came a blizzard, coming just the way
the sodden coffee grounds had been portending.
And once it came, it ceased to be impending.
That year December ended after only twenty days.

And taking off her overcoat, her hat
and gloves, she then unwound her wine-red scarf
and tossed her shawl onto the hearth,
then slowly, penitently dropped to kiss his hand.

As soon as she dropped down, her gaze was brushed
clean of its memory, then turned into a quarter
to six and subsequently crossed the border
to greet the dawn, which quite resembled dusk.

Her new gaze was a blazing path that reached
from her two eyes to his two sleeping eyes:
a path that she had once heard prophesied
as conquering insomnia and grief.

*　*　*

Ещё один e-mail в государство хаоса,
где крест с распятием висит в еврейском доме,
а член встаёт реже, чем дыбом волосы.

Увы, но в нём не осталось адресатов, кроме
вынужденных уйти из школы учителей
и проворовавшихся хороших знакомых.

На настоящий день, каких-то семь тысяч дней
спустя, жизнь в нём расползлась на мнения:
Кому-то живётся лучше, кому-то — веселей.

Одни читают Данте, другие — Маринину.
Одни стремятся на юг, другие поносят Запад.
Все вместе они согласны, но не знают, с чем именно.

Ещё один e-mail в государство, на год
отставшее от Цельсия и облаков,
вдоль которых летает белый аист.

...e-mail из разбросанных фраз и случайных слов,
не возвращающихся назад,
                                    как из воздуха
не возвращаются посланные пули.

...в государство, где после ратного подвига
Иван лежит на печи и мысленно рисует
картину, чей сюжет давно не нов.

* * *

One more e-mail to the state of chaos,
where a crucifix hangs in a Jewish home
and erections are rarer than electric shocks.

Alas, there's no one left to send this to, except
teachers who were forced to leave school
and good friends who were caught stealing.

As of the present day, some seven thousand days
later, life has unraveled into opinions:
Sóme folks are living better, some are having more fun.

Some read Dante, others Marinina mystery novels.
Some want to fly south, others rail against the West.
They all agree, but they don't know on what exactly.

One more e-mail to the state that's taken a year's
vacation from Celsius and clouds
along which a white stork is flying.

...an e-mail of tossed-out phrases and random words
that don't come back from the air,
                              like purposefully launched
bullets don't come back.

... to the state where after glory in battle
Ivan lies on the stove and draws a mental
picture of a subject that has long lost its novelty.

ПУЭРТОРИКАНСКИЙ ДНЕВНИК

Биане

I. Четверг, 2 июля, 11:30 утра

Атлантический берег.
Изобилие света.
Гордо высятся пальмы.
Что-то по Фаренгейту.
Мозг растерян.
Ни души для беседы.
Лишь туристы да хамы.
И песок без зонтов и скамеек.

Невесомость.
Соль впивается в спину.
Торс плывёт, как баранка.
Лиц не видно.
Визги сжаты в звук эха.
Небо вместо панамки.
Простота в замедленном темпе.
Невесомость.

Стая рыб — красных, жёлтых.
Океанская зелень.
Бледный профиль медузы.
Жизнь течёт еле-еле.
Жизни мало.
И подобие груза
в форме плавленой пены устало
упирается в воздух.

PUERTO RICAN DIARY

To Biana

I. Thursday, July 2, 11:30 am

Here it is — the Atlantic.
An abundance of light.
The palms tower proudly.
Some degrees Fahrenheit.
My thoughts are erratic.
Not a soul I can talk to.
Just tourists and jerks.
And sand — no umbrellas or benches.

Weightlessness.
Spine stinging with salt.
Torso afloat like a doughnut.
Not a face to be seen.
Shrieks compressed into an echo.
A sky in place of a sombrero.
Simplicity drifting in slo-mo.
Weightlessness.

Schools of fish — red and yellow.
Seaweed trolling the ocean.
A pale jellyfish profile.
Life just barely in motion.
Life existing just barely.
And a ponderous snowpile
of molten white seafoam is wearily
leaning into the air.

II. Четверг, 2 июля, вечером
(у памятника Колумбу)

Никто не ведает, как он конкретно выглядел.
Но он стоит, застыв с крестом в руке.
Коль вспомнить стелу В. И. Ленину в Москве,
то он в свои пятьсот —
                                        бесспорно вылитый
вождь нации, творец её истории:
сюда приплыл, вот здесь сказал,
                                                    а там построил.

Вот он стоит, с чертами главного героя
былых столетий, озирая море и
богатый брег (его леса, его поля),
как некогда стоял у мачт флотилии
с большевиками, курсом на Бастилию,
крича им по-испански: «На хуй, бля!»

Вот он стоит, предположительно уставший
от глаз туристов, порицающих Америку.
Вокруг — Пуэрто Рико и эстетика
бездарной жизни: грязной, нищей, павшей,
униженной вконец борьбой за мир
и верой в королеву и империю.

Никто не ведает ни духом, ни материей,
изношенной Базаровым до дыр,
какой должна быть жизнь и нужно ль бронзой
её заканчивать иль неким воскресением.
Он не был в этом смысле исключением,
пусть и застыл в почти надмирной позе.

II. Thursday, July 2, Evening
(at the Columbus monument)

Nobody knows exactly what he looked like.
But he stands frozen with a cross in hand.
Resembling Lenin's obelisk in Moscow,
His pose of these five hundred years
                              unquestionably struck like
the leader of a nation, creator of its history:
here's where he docked, said such-and-such,
                              built this fort here.

He stands there with the features of a hero
of bygone centuries, watching the sea roll
surveying a port so rich with forests and wild grasses,
as once he stood commanding a flotilla
of Bolsheviks, his sights on the Bastille,
yelling in Spanish: "Up your fucking asses!"

He stands, presumably bone tired
of eyes of tourists putting down America.
Around him Puerto Rico and the esthetic of
a mediocre life: poor, dirty, uninspired,
degraded by the fight for world dominion
and loyalty to queen and empire.

Nobody knows, by faith or numerous empirical
tests of Bazarov's nihilist opinions,
what life should be, and whether it should end in
bronze or some sort of resurrection.
In this sense, he was no exception,
although the pose he froze in looks almost transcendent.

Здесь он стоит, как некто, кто познал
вкус власти и тем вкусом не пресытился.
Он рвётся ввысь, не без излишнего неистовства
топча ногами обветшалый пьедестал.
Он рвётся ввысь, по постулатам вертикали
жизнь новую ища, а с ней — и новый вкус

деяний светлых, по которым стонет Русь,
валяясь на печи, храпя на сеновале.
Он рвётся ввысь, а прочие не ведают:
шагают мимо, пьют текилу, дышат влажностью.
И море чёрное шипит с плебейской важностью.
И Чацкий вдалеке кричит:
                    «Карету мне!»

III. Пятница, 3 июля, ближе к полудню
(из Мандельштама)

Мы шли по берегу. Витийствовало море.
День проступал на небе дымом, пеплом.
Гремел прибой: его шестнадцатые доли
сравнимы были с гневом Федры.

IV. Пятница, 3 июля, 8 вечера

Буквально двадцать-двадцать пять евреев.
Фактически евреев нет.
Зато есть синагога, в яркий цвет,
как старая еврейка, выкрашенная.
Скучища смертная… Шабат. На месте перьев
индейских — белые и синие ермолки,
сидящие вигвамами на лысых

He stands here, like someone who got a taste
of power, but was not completely satisfied.
He strains aloft, pumped up with extra rabid pride,
stamping his feet on a pedestal that's seen better days.
Defying verticality, he strains aloft,
seeks a new life — and with it, a new taste

of shining deeds that backward Russia moaningly awaits,
splayed on a stove and sleeping in a hayloft.
He strains aloft, and no one has a clue:
they walk past, drink tequila, breathe in the humidity.
The black sea fizzes with plebeian tumidity
And somewhere Chatsky calls:
                    "A carriage — get me out of here!"

III. Friday, July 3, close to noon
(after Mandelshtam)

We walked along the shore. The sea waxed eloquent.
Day filtered through the sky like smoke, like ash.
The breakers rumbled: their persistent sixteenth beats
comparable to Phaedra's wrath.

IV. Friday, July 3, 8 pm

Literally twenty or twenty-five Jews.
Practically no Jews at all.
There's a synagogue, though, all dolled
up in bright colors, like an old Jewish lady.
What mortal boredom... It's Shabbat. White and blue
striped yarmulkes in place of Indian feathers
perched on bald

и южных головах.
Беспечной радости на лицах
не менее, чем в розовом вине.
Войди Аллах
сюда, он тоже облачился бы в ермолку
и рассмеялся бы, как не
написано в Коране.

Пора молиться, но так жарко, что не тянет.

Беспечный ребе произносит с пляжной леностью:
«Алейну — на странице сорок шесть».
Все поднимаются, застряв меж сном и вечностью.
Возможно, вечность вправду есть,
но для чего тогда молитвы, если в смертном
общении сего не подтвердить?
Никто не знает ничего. Лишь остаётся
нашёптывать, гнусавить, голосить
и, в такт другим евреям,
из слов чеканить веру.

Скучища смертная... Бежать, бежать скорее!
Бежать — конечно, но куда?
На этом острове так много от Христа,
что, верно, чувствуешь себя примером
вороны белокурой. Сам Христос
невольно где-то рядом — бродит, действуя
кому-нибудь на нервы. В синагогу
войди сейчас он в чёрной шляпе, с пейсами,
то рассмеялся бы, призвав себе в подмогу
цитату из Матвея или Марка.

southern heads like wigwams.
Carefree joy on their faces
as plentiful as rosé wine.
Should Allah come
in here, he'd put on a yarmulke too
and burst out laughing like he
never does in the Qur'an.

It's time to pray, but so hot you can barely stand.

The carefree rabbi announces with beach-bum solemnity:
"*Aleinu* — page forty-six."
Everyone rises, caught between sleep and eternity.
It's possible eternity truly exists,
but then why pray if mortal
interaction can't confirm it?
No one knows anything. All you can do
is mutter, snuffle, blurt
in time with other Jews,
coaxing faith from words.

What mortal boredom... I've got to run, run, quickly as I can!
Run, of course — but where?
There's so much of Christ on this island
that you really feel like a quintessential
white raven. Christ himself
is randomly wandering someplace nearby, getting
on someone's nerves. Should he happen by the synagogue
and come in right now in a black hat and payos,
he'd burst out laughing, calling for backup
with a quote from Matthew or Mark.

Безумно жарко.
Да, пора молиться.
Молиться при Аллахе и Христе,
еврейские рассматривая лица.
Буквально двадцать-двадцать пять типичных лиц,
хранящих ашкеназскую Европу
под этим солнцем, в этой духоте.

Евреев, вроде, нет, но также нет столиц,
в которых нет евреев.
И Сан-Хуан не исключенье, господа.
А то, что скучно — что ж, пусть свист Борея
разгонит скуку, приглашая холода
на смену Фаренгейту нынешнему…
Вот так.
И это всё!
Хвала Всевышнему!

V. Суббота, 4 июля, рано утром

Мы празднуем четвёртое июля
сегодня на окраине страны.
Без фейерверков, без звучанья увертюры
Чайковского, покорной тишиной
врасплох захваченные, будто тишины
должно быть ровно столько, сколько ныне:
не больше и не меньше.

С патриотизмом здесь, по счастью, скверно.
Во-первых, — слишком знойно. Во-вторых, —
лень, скука и медлительность. Наверно,
сие освобождает от грехов,
особенно четвёртого июля.

It's hot enough to go berserk.
All right, it's time to pray.
Let us pray in the presence of Allah and Christ,
looking around at Jewish faces.
Literally twenty or twenty-five faces
preserving Ashkenazic Europe
under this sun, in this stifling heat.

There are no Jews to speak of, but there are no capitals
where there are no Jews.
And San Juan is no exception, truth be told.
But it's so boring — if only a boreal blast
would chase away the boredom, inviting in the cold
to make this current Fahrenheit be
gone. Poof!
That would be that.
Praise be to the Almighty!

V. Saturday, July 4, early morning

We're celebrating Independence Day
secluded at the country's outer edge.
No fireworks or Tchaikovsky's "1812".
Caught unawares by a submissive silence,
as though the recommended daily dose of silence
should be exactly what it is today:
no more, no less.

Luckily, patriotism doesn't thrive here.
First off, it's too darn hot. And secondly,
the soul grows idle, bored and sluggish. This
may very well absolve it of its sins,
especially this fourth day of July.

Даруй мне жизнь другое измеренье,
я отплатил бы ей, прожив вне США
и вне России, расставляя ударенья
над прежними слогами, но со скоростью
иною, ибо скоростью душа
определяет запылённый угол стрелок
на циферблате.

Я стою без плавок
на каменном балконе, с видом на
классическое море и три пляжа.
Приехав на окраину страны,
стою и ставлю двоеточие: страна
меня кормила и поила — я же, будто
анти-Овидий, прибыл добровольно.
При этом тороплюсь и *за* окраину —
узнать что там и как, — коль будет судно.
И думаю, что будет. Но куда ж
нам плыть?.. Да, думаю, что будет.

VI. Суббота, 4 июля, после захода солнца

Каяки разбивают темноту,
как лёд — форель.
Пуэрто-Рико путеводным ветром направляет
ближайшую звезду,
но бесполезно — ночь.
Из осязаемых вещей —
лишь ночь и ветер, дующий на запад,
подавшийся из мест восточных прочь
от жизни полупрожитой.

Were life to grant me one more incarnation,
I'd gladly live my days outside the USA
and outside Russia, too, pronouncing my orations
in the same rhythm, only at a different
speed — for what the soul would designate
as speed is just the dust-caked angle of the hands
on a clockface.

I stand with no swim trunks
looking out from a stone-arched balcony
upon a classic sea and three white beaches.
Having arrived at the edge of the country
I stand and plant a colon: that's the country
that brought me up and fed me — yet I came here, like some
anti-Ovid, of my own free will.
And now I itch to go *beyond* the edge —
to know what's out there — I just need to find a ship.
And I believe I will. But where on earth
are we to sail?... I do believe we will.

VI. Saturday, July 4, after sunset

Kayaks are breaking through the dark
like trout through ice.
The Puerto Rican guiding wind is trying mightily
to steer the nearest star,
but to no avail — it's night.
Of all things tangible to us
there's only night and headwinds blowing westward
from places where the sun is on the rise,
away from lives half-lived.

Молчит лагуна. Липнут к водорослям вёсла.
Лежит змея. Бездействуют цикады.
Каяки разбивают темноту,
двухлопастным прямоугольным стадом
сужаясь меж чащоб.
Здесь ты плывёшь, здесь я плыву,
насколько могут по обители теней плыть
                                    двое смертных.

И по спине озноб,
и девяносто пять по Фаренгейту,
и взгляд Вергилия.

И дальше — взгляды, что узреть не суждено:
Электры, Гектора, Энея.
И — уши, кои слышат лишь одно
и то же: от Платона, Диогена.
И профиль Птолемея,
и силуэт Эвклида.
И поднимается невидимая пена,
пока каяки разбивают темноту
искусственно, надуманно, для вида
и на виду
у Вечности.

VII. Воскресенье, 5 июля, 10 утра

1

Удивительно, как быстро
надоедает остров.
Его отель, его история, его нехватка чая.
Лежать под солнцем, сонно небо замечая, —
вот весь удел.

The dark lagoon is silent. Paddles stick to water lilies.
The snake lies still. Cicadas stop their buzzing.
The kayaks breaking through the dark,
a double-bladed rectilinear flock, are squeezing
their way through underbrush.
And you are swimming, I am swimming,
as far as the realm of shadows can be swum
                                        by two mere mortals.
Along our backs a shivered hush
and ninety-seven Fahrenheit
and Virgil's guiding gaze.

And onward — gazes fated never to see the light
though they beheld the rise of Troy:
Electra, Hector and Aeneas.
And ears attuned to the master of those who learned
from Plato and Diogenes
and charted the course to Euclid and Ptolemy.
And foam ascends unseen
as kayaks breaking through the dark
take measured, studied oarstrokes for a view
and in the view
of Eternity.

VII. Sunday, July 5, 10 am

1

It's amazing how quickly
an island gets dull.
The hotel, the history, the lack of tea.
Lying in the sun, eyeing the sky sleepily —
that's all there is to do.

2

Чем больше времени на острове, тем меньше
на ум приходит прилагательных.
Чем меньше прилагательных, тем меньше
причин воздать Создателю
за море и песок, за горизонт и берег.

3

Весь остров двуязычен, но ни на
одном из двух нет воли разговаривать.
Меж мыслью и произнесённым словом — марево
из тишины. Я полагаю, тишина —
синоним двуязычия.

4

Вот весь удел: лежать полдня под солнцем,
как прочие четыре миллиона душ
на острове, взгляд развлекая плотским
пространством неба, усмехаясь изредка:
«Какого чёрта я забрался в эту глушь?»

VIII. Воскресенье, 5 июля, 6 вечера

Если то — не прибой
и не шум душевой,
если то — не ничьей
ставшей лейка с водой,
то тогда — это сны.

Если то — не песок,
не скольжение ног,
если то — не ожог,
то тогда — это сны.

The more time on an island, the fewer
adjectives come to mind.
The fewer adjectives, the fewer
reasons to thank the Divine
for sea and sand, for shoreline and horizon.

The whole island is bilingual, but there's just
no urge to talk in either one.
Between the thought and the uttered word is hazy dust
of silence. I guess silence
is a synonym for bilingualism.

That's all there is: you lie for half the day in the infernal
sun, like the four million other souls
on the island, feasting your eyes on the carnal
expanse of sky, chuckling once in a while:
"How the hell did I land in this forsaken hole?"

VIII. Sunday, July 5, 6 pm

If it's not the waves' power
at the high tidal hour
or the hiss of a shower
or a pail left unscoured,
then it must be a dream.

If it's not grains of sand
slipping through open hands
onto legs overtanned,
then it must be a dream.

Если то — не твой взгляд
при бездействии ватт,
то тогда — это сны.

Если то — не вина,
то тогда — это сны.

То тогда — сны, только сны, не более.

If it isn't your gaze
in the salt marshes' haze,
then it must be a dream.

If it's nobody's fault,
then it must be a dream.

Then it must be a dream, just a dream, nothing more.

Вот Пушкин пишет ровным ямбом, что «иных
    уж нет, а те далече».
Вот Сталин думает опять на «Турбиных»
    сходить в свободный вечер.
Вот Рихтер в Зальцбурге играет «ХТК»,
    а Моцарт в птичьей гамме
летит, попутно рассекая облака
    и плачет с облаками.

Пойдём на ужин, милый друг, и вспомним всех,
    кто упомянут выше.
Ты им писал когда-то письма — что не грех,
    а способ выжить в нише.
Возможно, таинство души и ремесла
    хранит не речь — бумага,
как часть той силы, что желает вечно зла,
    но совершает благо.

As Pushkin writes in neat iambic verse: "Some are
    no more, and others far away."
And Stalin thinks of going out to see "White Guards"
    again after a busy day.
And Richter plays in Salzburg, his technique well tempered,
    And Mozart scales the clouds
like birds that keep on singing in a springtime tempest
    and sheds tears with the clouds.

Let's go and dine, dear friend, and then we will recall
    each one, the classic and romantic.
You used to write them letters, which is no sin at all —
    It's a survival tactic.
The mysteries of the soul, the secrets of the guild
    may not be told aloud, but could
be kept on paper, like a force forever wishing ill
    that ends up doing good.

НА УРОКАХ РУССКОЙ ЛИТЕРАТУРЫ

I

Лара захлопнула дверцу и крикнула: «Солнце
девственно слепит застенчивым
                                         зайчиком лета.
Завтра исчезнет, и, значит, уехать придётся
в город, где улицы славятся вечным рассветом».

Только захлопнула —
                    Ларе припомнился Марбург:
птицы над куполом, книги в кафе, смех в аллеях.
И как виднелся из окон распахнутых замок
в скалах, где шёпотом пела юнцам Лорелея.

«Значит, уедем туда! Пусть война, пусть неверно
карты вещают пасьянсные.
                              Карты есть карты».
Ларе припомнился Марбург, и, некогда скверный,
запах перронов теперь показался приятным.

«Катю в охапку! Оставить письмо. Не сметь плакать!
Вещи в дорогу, что позже о солнце напомнят!»
Лара захлопнула дверцу. «И также оставить
опыт любви —
            самый первый осознанный опыт».

RUSSIAN LITERATURE CLASSES

I

Lara slammed shut the door, shouting: "The sun is demurely
bouncing off summer like snowdrifts,
                                    its bashful light blinding.
It will be gone by tomorrow, which means we must surely
move to a town where the sun is eternally rising."

Just as she slammed the door,
                        Lara remembered old Marburg:
birds on a cupola, books in cafés, tree-lined laughter.
Windows thrown open, revealing a castle held guard by
rocks where fair Lorelei sang to young men on the water.

"That's where we'll go! Never mind there's a war on, and
never mind what the cards may foretell.
                        All we have is the present."
Lara remembered old Marburg... the squalid and heavy
train platform smell now surprisingly struck her as pleasant.

"Bundle up Katya! Just leave a goodbye note. No crying!
Let these bags store up the memory of sunlight for later."
Lara slammed shut the train door. "Now, just one last
goodbye to love —
            the first earthly experience we are aware of."

II

Внутри красного дома, между Парк и Лексингтон,
доживала свой век старуха из «Пиковой».
Она с трудом поднималась по паркетной лестнице
и стыдилась памяти, как своего титула.

Она плохо слышала окрики горничной
и безмолвно общалась с еврейским доктором.
Лишь на ветер, дующий с посвистом призрачным,
отвечала порой зловещим шёпотом.

Она помнила Германа: его профиль каменный,
его руки в сумраке, его поступь — помнила.
Он являлся к ней в снах со словами странными,
что-то там про карты,

                    всё вокруг да около.

Он являлся и исчезал всегда одинаково,
через заднюю дверь, заросшую вербою.
В темноте обменивался с кем-то знаками
и спешил прочь, на Семьдесят Первую.

II

In a stately red building between Park and Lexington,
the Queen of Spades lives out her years in tranquility.
She totters up the staircase in parqueted elegance,
ashamed of her memories and her nobility.

She has trouble hearing the shouts of her housekeeper
and communicates with her Jewish doctor wordlessly.
Only now and then, when a phantom wind howls at her,
does she make a response, menacingly murmuring.

She remembers Hermann: his stony countenance,
his hands in half-shadow, his steps in the anteroom.
He appears to her in dreams, speaking words
unaccountable — something strange about cards,
$\qquad\qquad\qquad$ with an importunate attitude.

He appears and disappears the same way consistently,
through the back door overgrown with shrubs soft and
leathery. In the darkness he signals to someone invisible
and then rushes off into the depths of the 70s.

СОНЕТ-ГАММА

В этой комнате дух с телом разлучён.
В этой комнате играет он.

Воском ухо расплавляя и шепча
медленно, здесь высится свеча.

Силуэт восходит плавно в тень
и рифмует с тенью божий день.

Шелест воздуха не проникает в слух,
ибо так задумал Бах.

Только Бах —
в этой комнате, где раньше длился страх.

В этой комнате, где око и рука
соединены одной

вертикалью, что ему наверняка
кажется кривой.

SONNET-SCALE

In this room body and soul part ways.
In this room he plays.

As its wax melts the ear and whispers soft
and slow, a candle holds its flame aloft.

A silhouette blends smoothly into gray
and rhymes with the godly light of day.

No whoosh of air will penetrate the ear,
for that was Bach's idea.

Only Bach is here
in this room, the erstwhile holding cell of fear.

In this room, eye and hand
are linked together by a plumb

line, whose path is spanned
by a pendulum.

ТУРЕЦКИЕ СТИХИ

Биане

I. Бегство в Константинополь

Ночь в проулках Стамбула,
на границе Европы,
растворяется в гуле
протяжной молитвы.

Ночь в проулках, и кошки
голосят, размножаясь
на ступенчатой крыше,
где свил гнездо аист.

Ночь, и голос Эфрона
в ожидании солнца
чётко и монотонно
откуда-то раздаётся.

То ли звук евразийства,
мусульманства дух то ли,
превращает убийство
в союз народа и воли.

То ли ночь и безумье
поменялись местами
так, чтоб в уличном шуме
услышать «Бог с вами».

TURKISH VERSES

To Biana

I. Fleeing to Constantinople

Night in Istanbul's alleys
on the border of Europe
dissolves in a volley
of clamorous prayer.

In the alleys the cats
vocalize, multiplying
atop a stepped roof
where a stork's nest is hiding.

And the lone voice of Efron
as he waits for the sun
comes from some vague direction
in a clear monotone.

Did the call of Eurasia
or the spirit of Islam
bring forth a free nation
from a murderous kingdom?

Or has night traded places
with madness, to wish you
amid the streets' chaos
a fond "God be with you"?

II. Смирна 1922

С заходом солнца в Измире доносятся крики армян,
тех, что ждут корабли, волнуясь за горизонт.
Город невидим в пыли, две недели как сдан:
подавлен христианский бунт.

Намечается вновь классический жанр резни
из красок кровавой бани вдоль берегов.
Вновь возможность с историей закончить дни
иль оказаться гонимым, как Иов.

В лучшем случае гонимым, ибо чужая земля
даёт шанс на подлинность сини вдали
и даёт подписаться под виденным: «Я,
дождавшийся корабля и этой земли».

III. Жара в Сельджуке

Какая-то чехарда. Какой-то там Эфес.
Какой-то волк, убежавший в лес.
Когда-то храм — теперь одна колонна.
И некогда жившая рядом мадонна.

Где нет туристов — там грядки и грязь.
Поэтому и яблоку негде упасть.
У древних камней — изобилие камер.
И вздохов тех, кто бездарно умер.

Капает дождь, будто гранатовый сок.
Толпятся жрецы: один среди них — Бог.
Во взгляде Бога немного Византии.
И некоторой ностальгии.

II. Smyrna 1922

As the sun sets in Izmir, it carries Armenians' shrieks —
from those awaiting ships, yearning to cross
away from this city engulfed in smoke: it's been two weeks
since the Christians made their stand and lost.

The classical genre of slaughter in all its misery
plays out once again as blood bathes the shores.
Again the prospect of ending one's days with history
or being cast out like Job, hungry and sore.

Better to be cast out, for an alien sky
gives a chance to see genuine azure first-hand
and bear witness to what you experienced: "I
survived to board a ship and see this land."

III. Heat in Selçuk

This used to be Ephesus? Ruins cheek by jowl.
Some tile with a bas-relief wolf on the prowl.
In place of a temple, a column — no more.
At one point the madonna lived somewhere next door.

Away from the tourists are gardens so small
that even an apple has nowhere to fall.
The ancient stones echo with chambers and sighs
of those within them who thanklessly died.

Rain drips like pomegranate juice.
God's face under a priest's hood — you never know whose.
There's a bit of Byzantium in God's gaze.
And a little nostalgia for bygone days.

* * *

И всё-таки в конце быть должен свет.
Да будет свет!
Чего угодно ради: души иль женских черт.

Пусть худосочная полоска света,
                                спускаясь с облаков,
не обратившихся в стену дождя,
                                проникнет в твой альков.
Пусть промелькнёт, не задерживаясь взглядом,
                                на каждом из
ночных предметов — то бегущей вверх,
                                то бегущей вниз.
Пусть осветит остатки паутины
                                и некоторые сны,
бежавшие от памяти в лоно
                                предутренней тишины.
И пусть на чём-нибудь остановится, хотя бы —
                                на песочных часах,
чтобы исчезнуть такой, какой была в облаках.

И это будет свет.
Именно таким будет свет.
Именно таким.

No matter what, in the end there should be light.
Let there be light!
For the sake of whatever: the soul or a woman's features.

Let an anemic strand of light,
                    trickling down from the clouds like a brook
that didn't turn into a wall of rain,
                                    filter into your nook.
Let it glimmer, not letting its glance linger,
                                    on every last
one of your nighttime objects — now running up,
                            now running down fast.
Let it light up the strands of a spiderweb
                            and some dreams drawn
from memory into the bosom of silence
                        that comes before dawn.
And let it settle somewhere,
                    even on the sand in a glass,
only to take on the form it had borne in the clouds, and pass.

And that will be light.
The light will be just like that.
Just like that.

Александр Вейцман пишет стихотворения и прозу на английском и русском языках. Автор нескольких книг. Его стихи, переводы, рассказы и эссе опубликованы более чем в пятидесяти журналах в разных уголках земного шара. Выпускник Гарвардского и Йельского университетов. Живёт в Нью-Йорке.

Alexander Veytsman writes poetry and prose in both English and Russian languages. He is the author of several books. His original poems, translations, as well as short stories and essays, have appeared in more than fifty publications worldwide. A graduate of Harvard and Yale universities, Alexander lives in New York City.

Лоренс Богослав — директор издательства East View Press и соучредитель Миннесотской лаборатории перевода для эмигрантов и беженцев. Вёл курсы русского языка и перевода в нескольких университетах. Регулярно выступает с лекциями на темы перевода, культуры, литературы и журналистики.

Laurence Bogoslaw is the director of East View Press and a co-founder of the Minnesota Translation Laboratory, a community language service for immigrants and refugees. He has taught Russian and translation courses at various universities. In addition, he regularly gives presentations on translation, culture, literature and journalism.